Cueva de los Verdes:

For centuries, this cave in Lanzarote was used by local inhabitants as a hideout to protect themselves from pirate attacks.

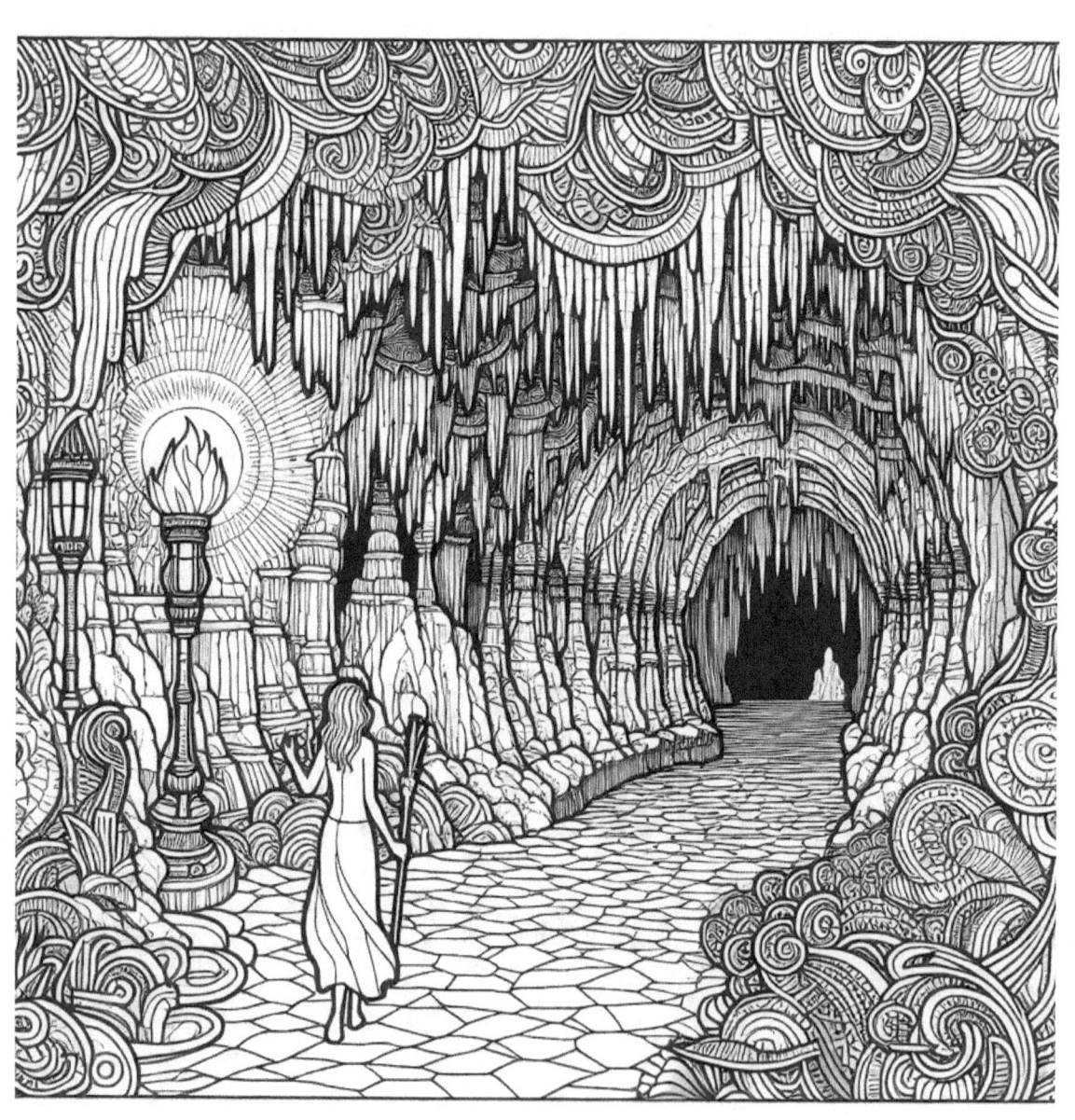

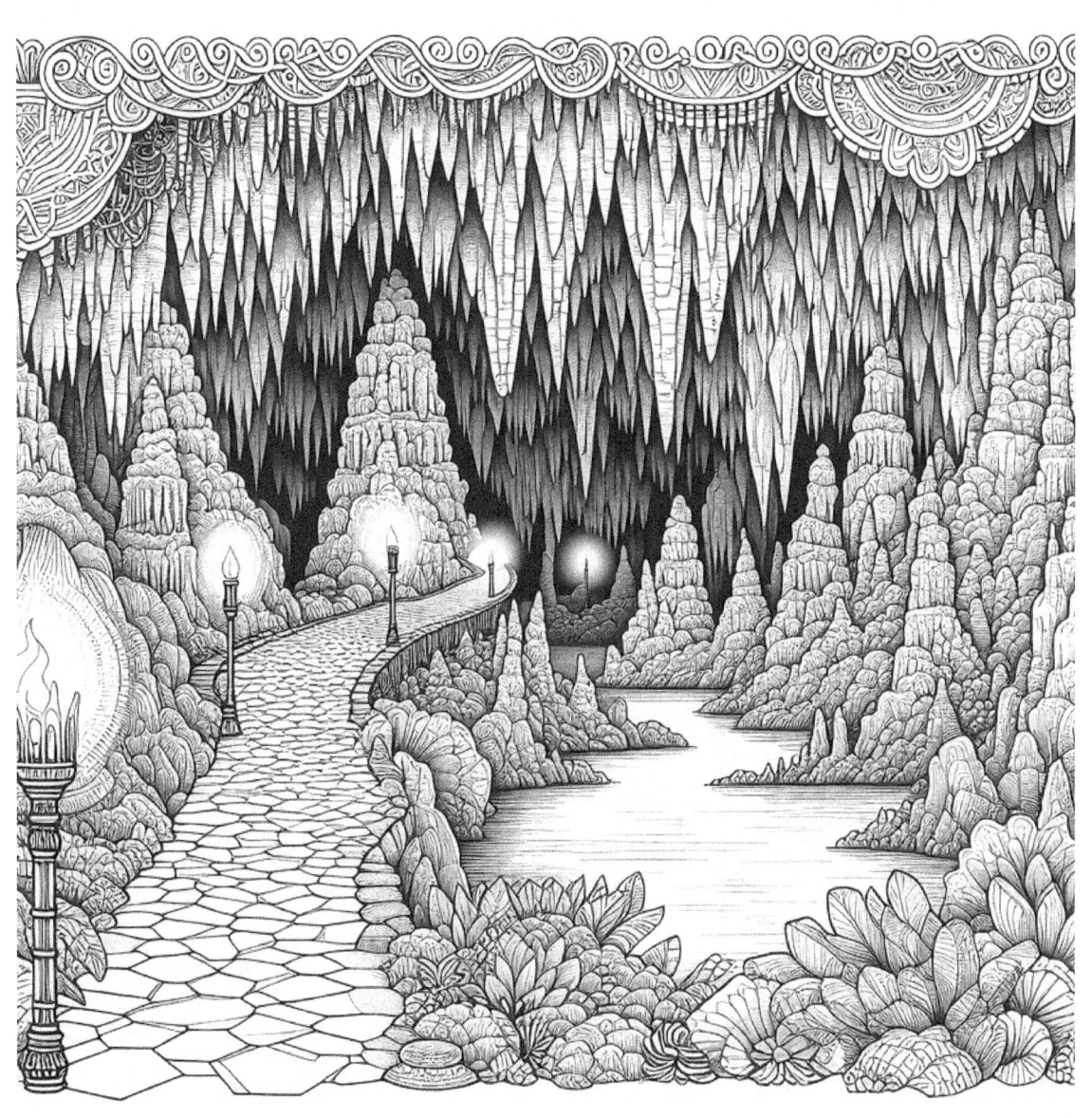

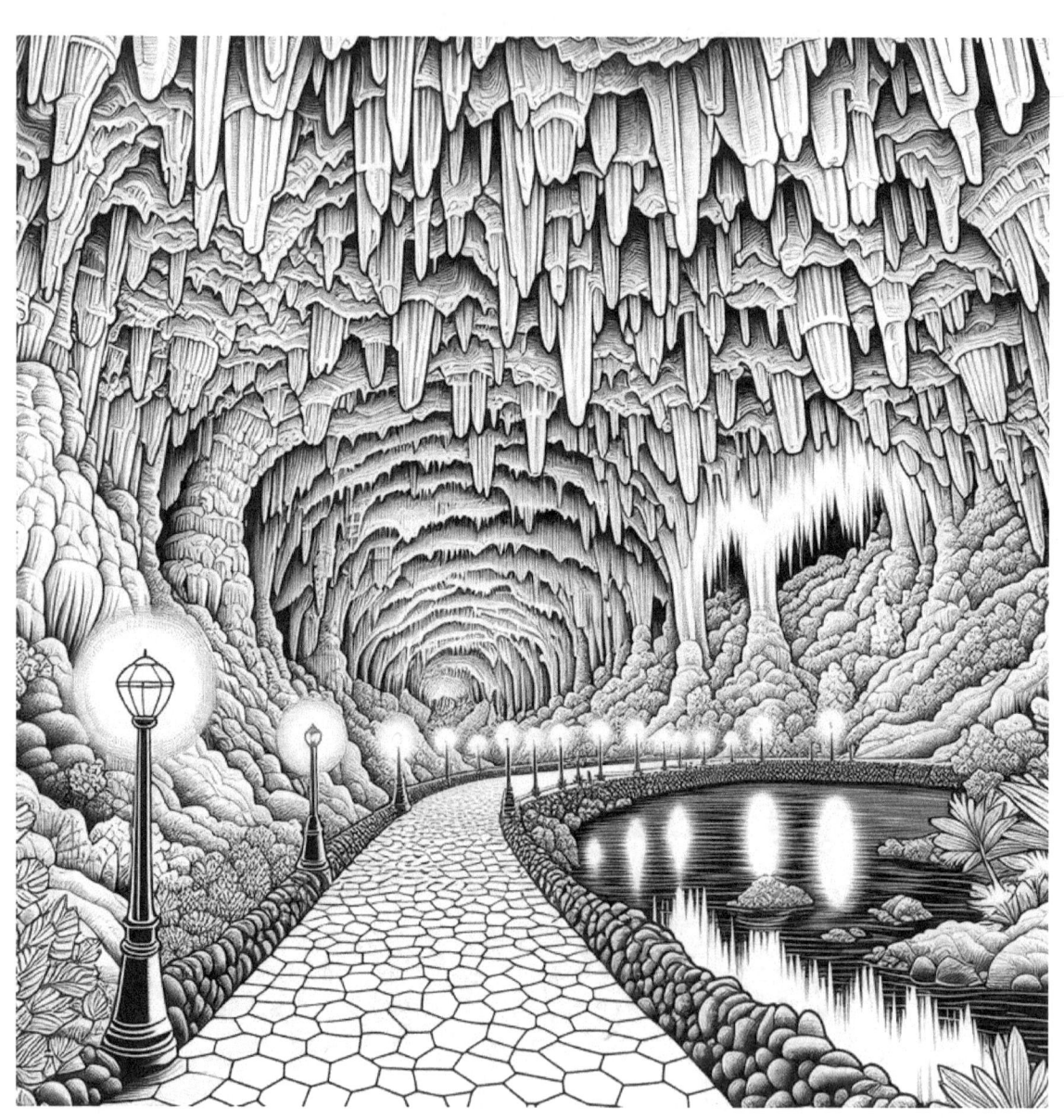

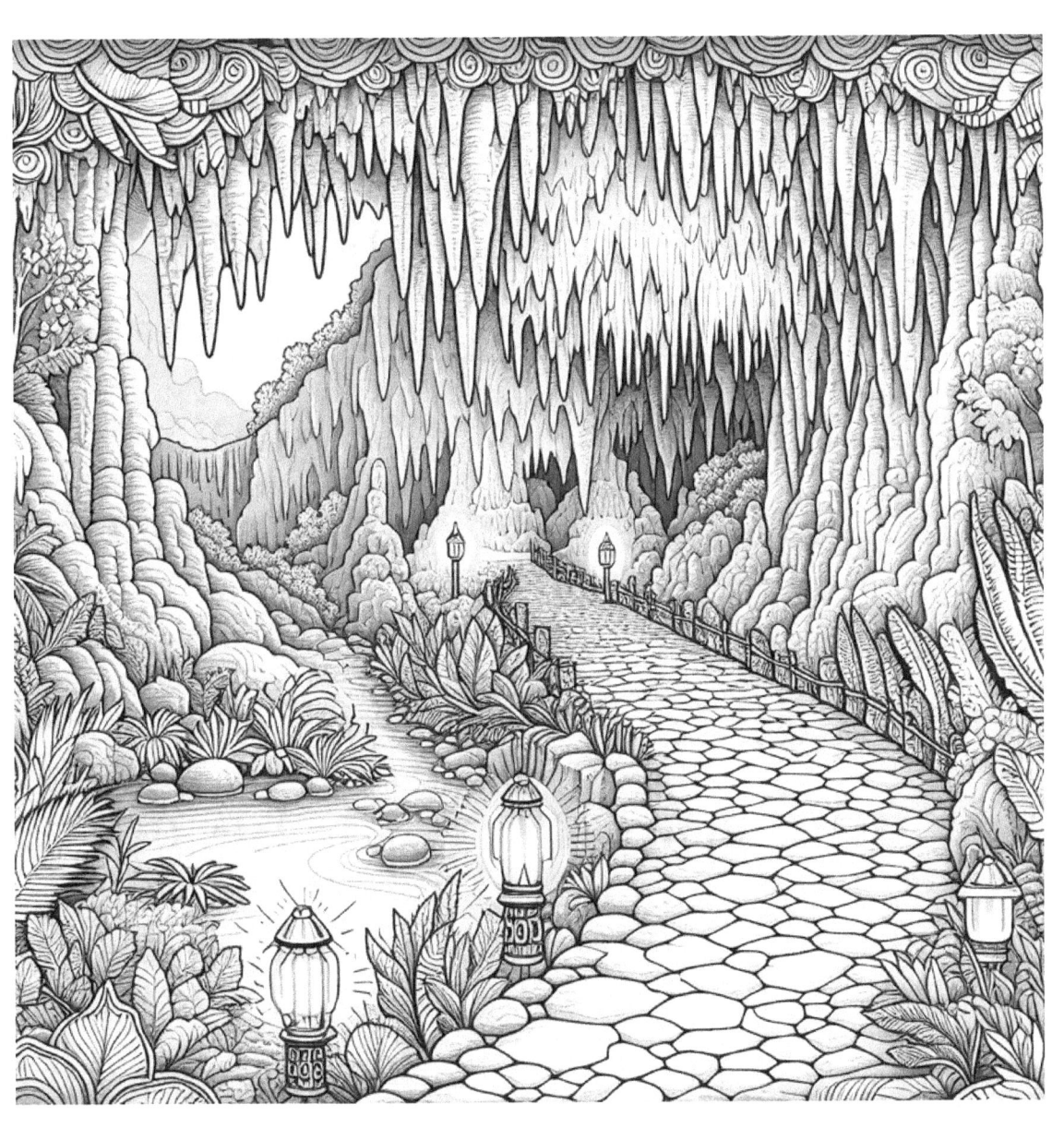

Parque Nacional de Timanfaya:

Despite its inhospitable appearance, some species of plants and animals have managed to adapt to the harsh volcanic conditions of the park.

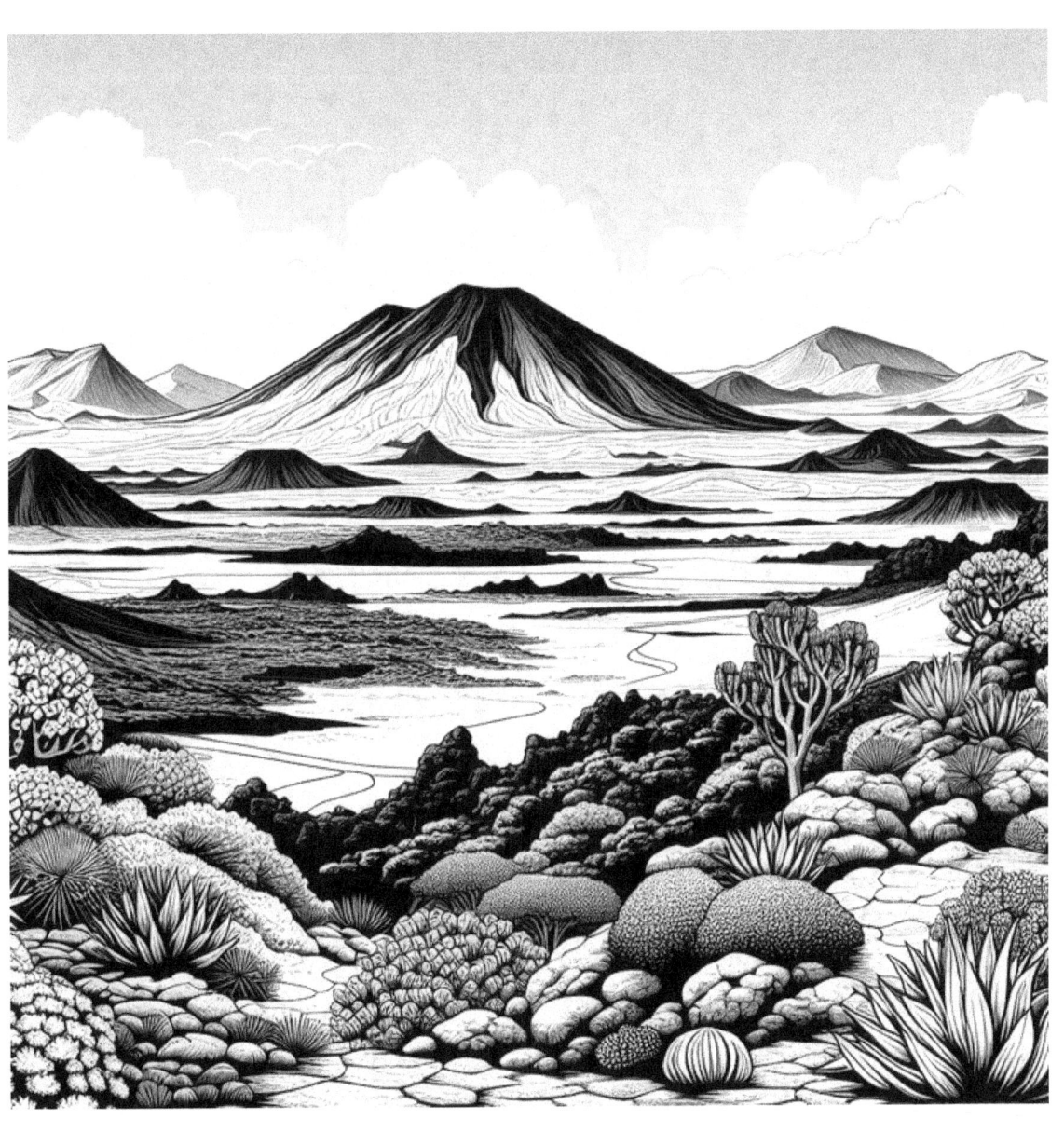

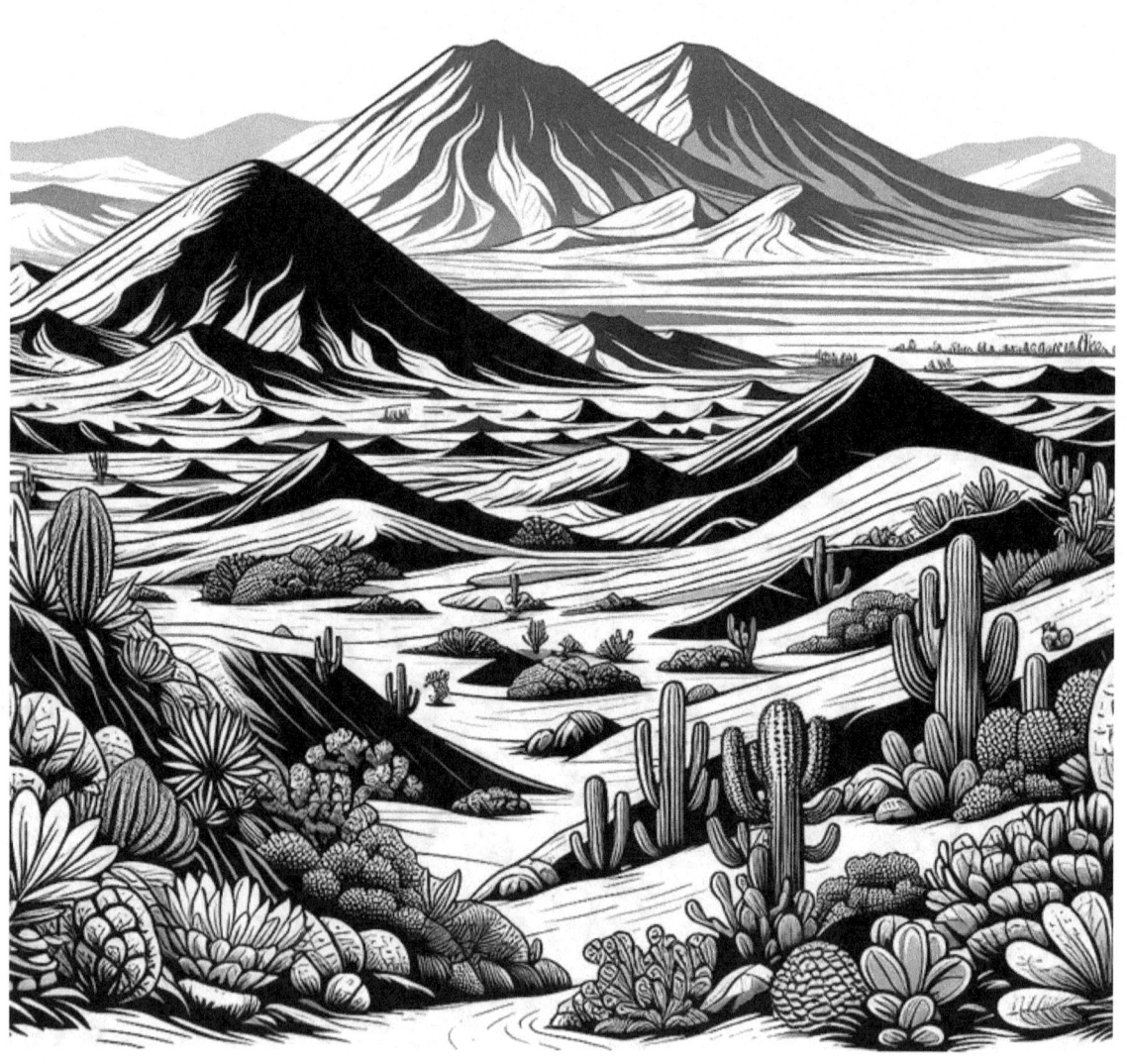

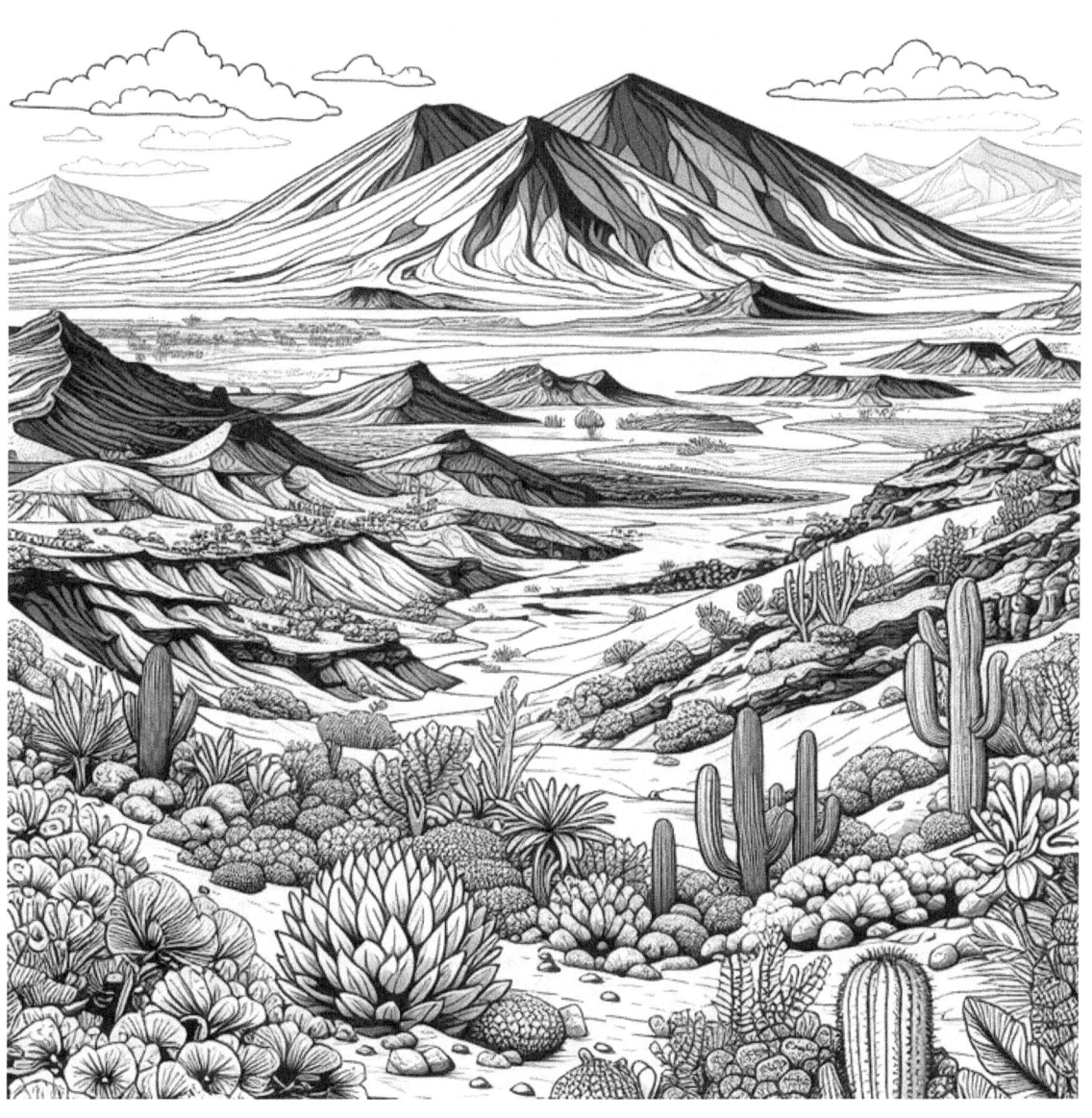

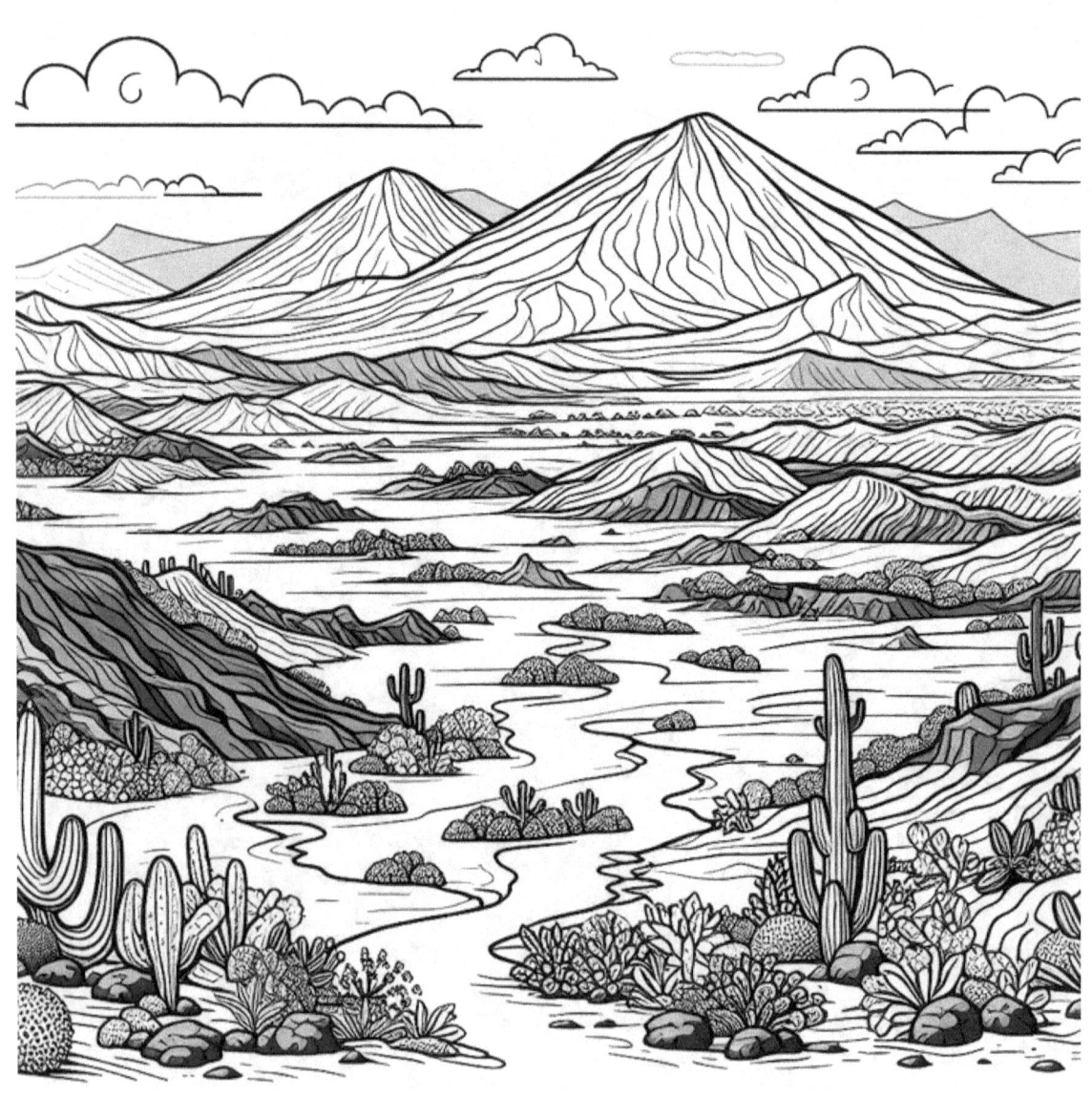

Las Médulas:

During the Roman era, it is estimated that around 1.6 million kilograms of gold were extracted from these mines, leaving behind a spectacular landscape.

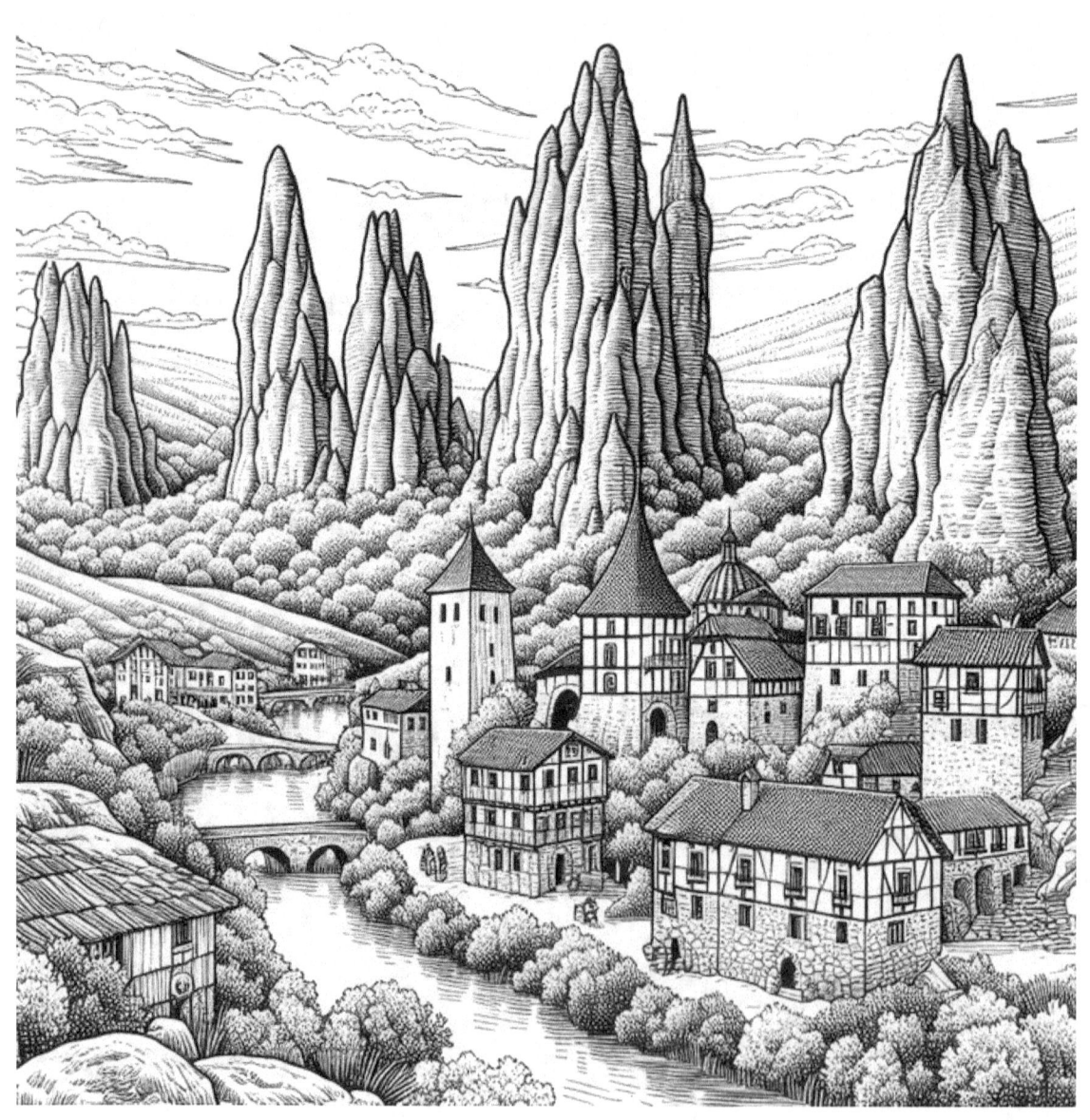

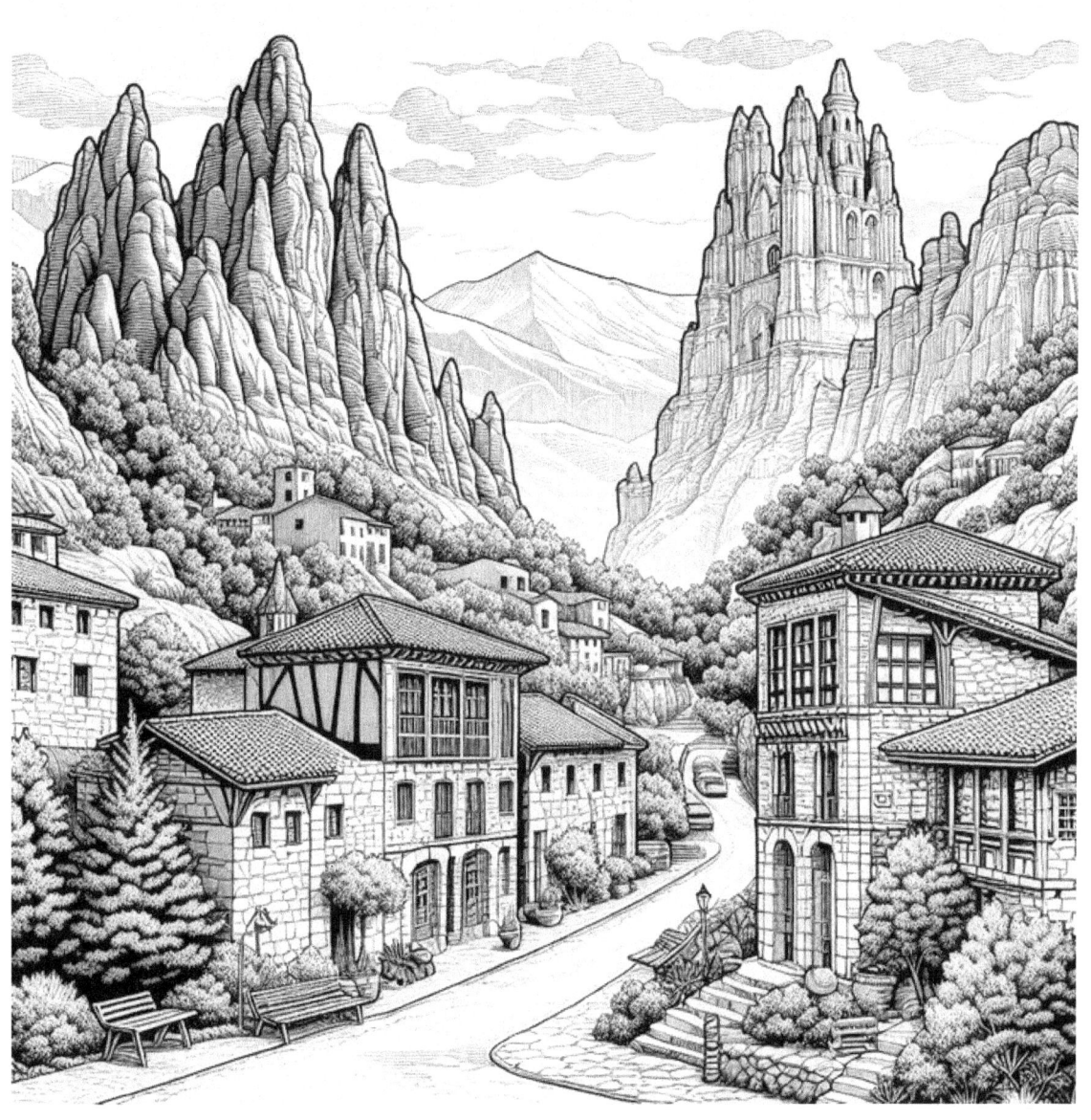

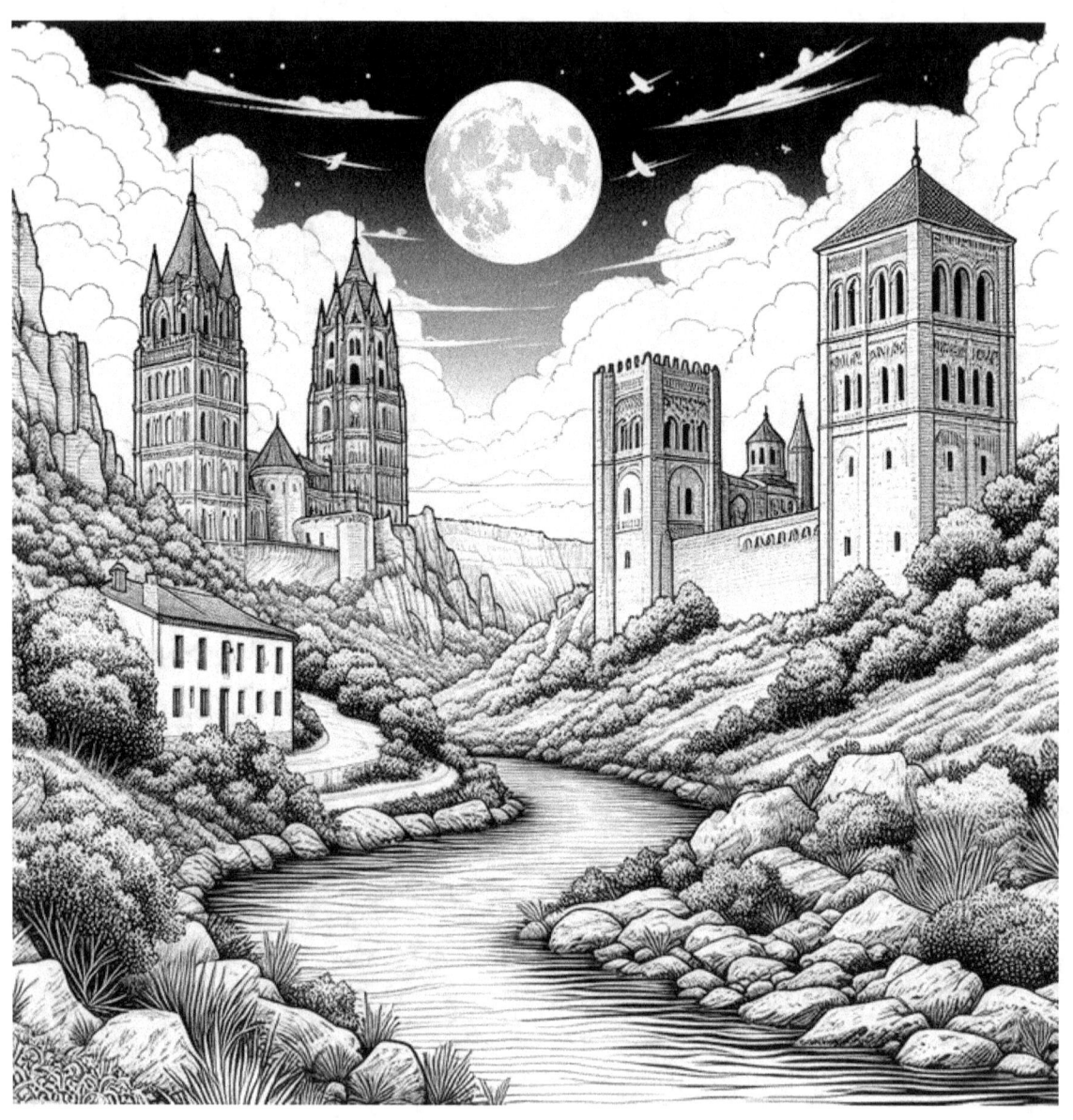

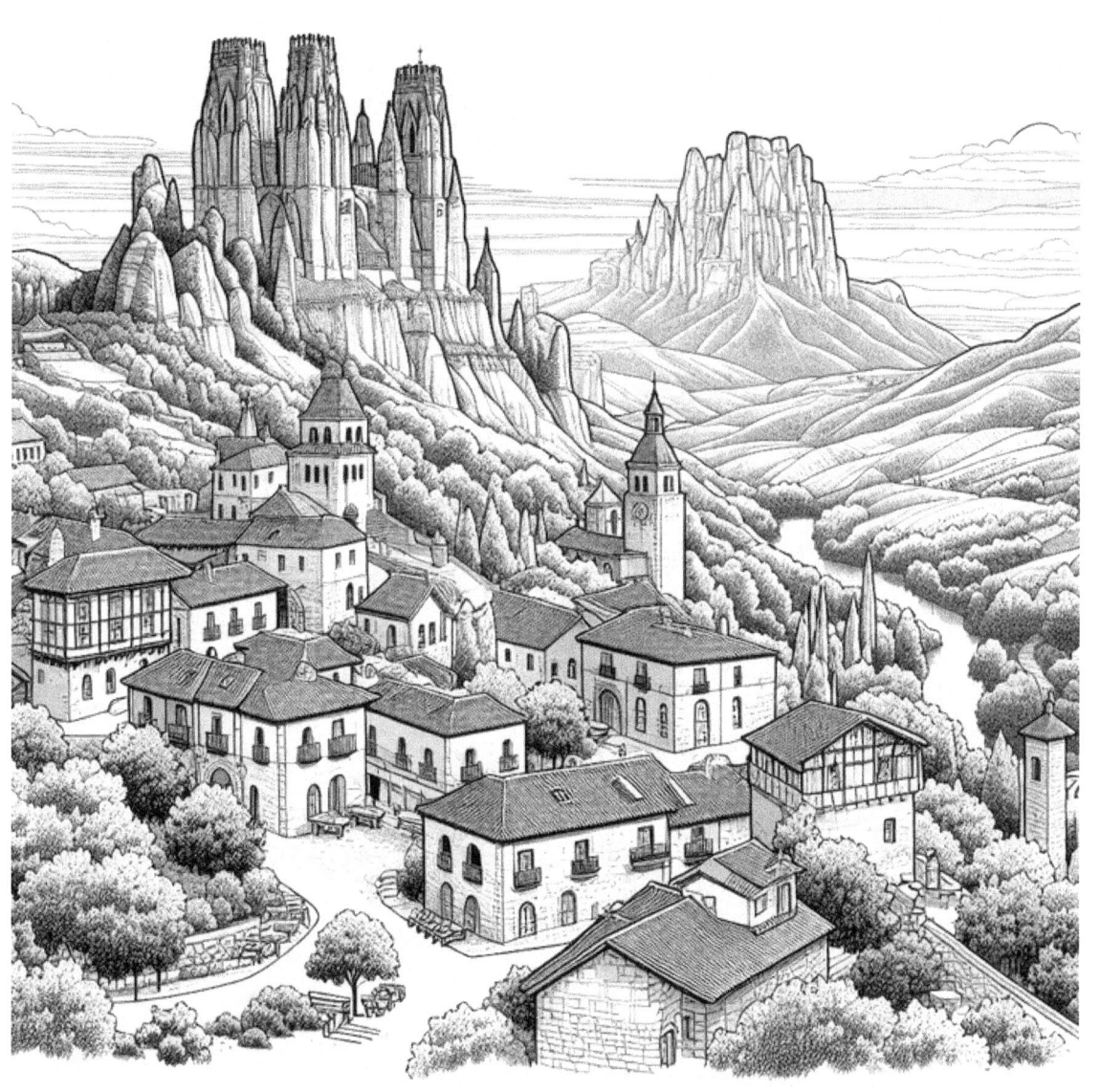

Parque Nacional de Aigüestortes y Lago de San Mauricio:

It harbors a great diversity of flora and fauna, including species such as the bearded vulture and the capercaillie.

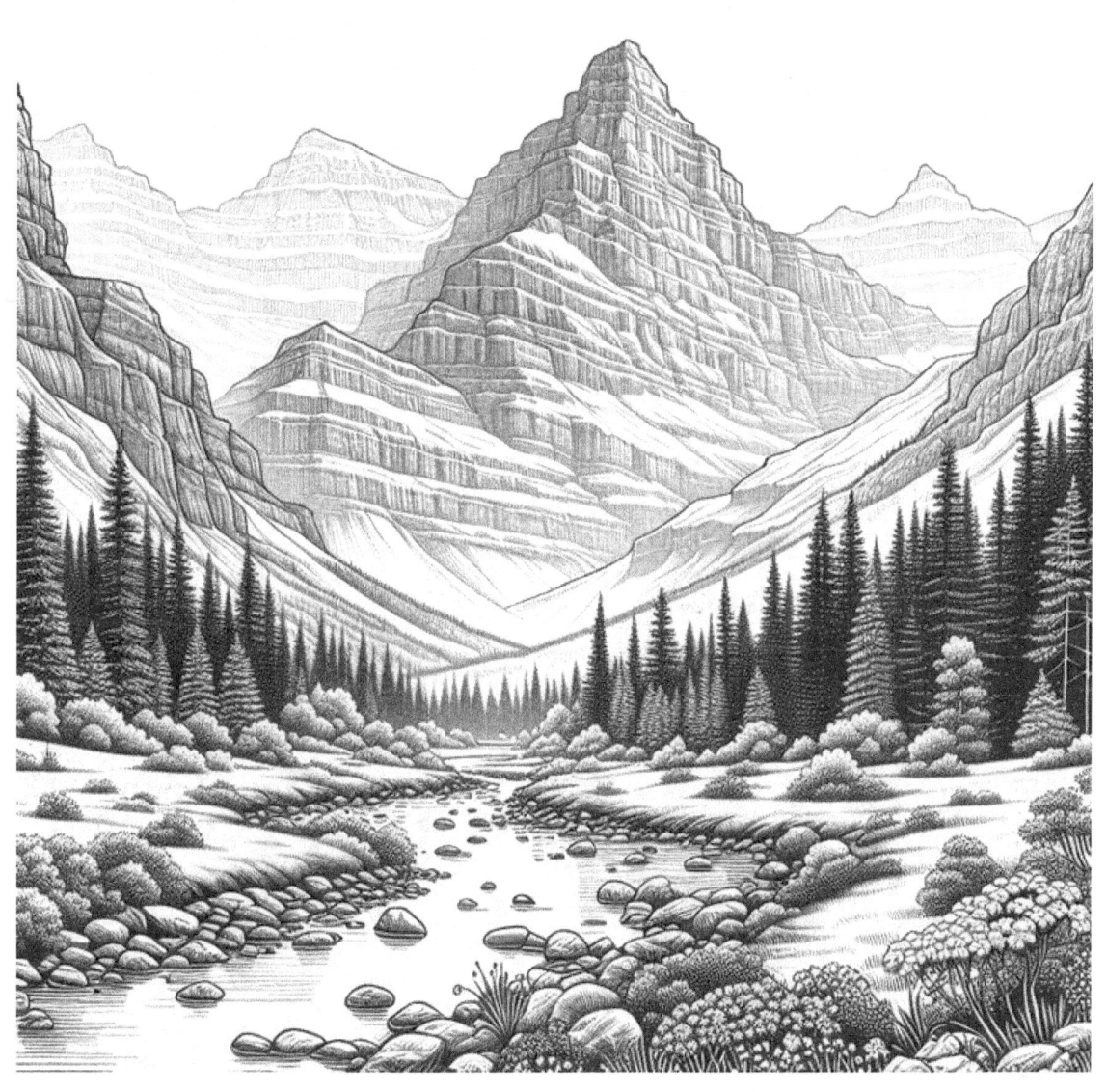

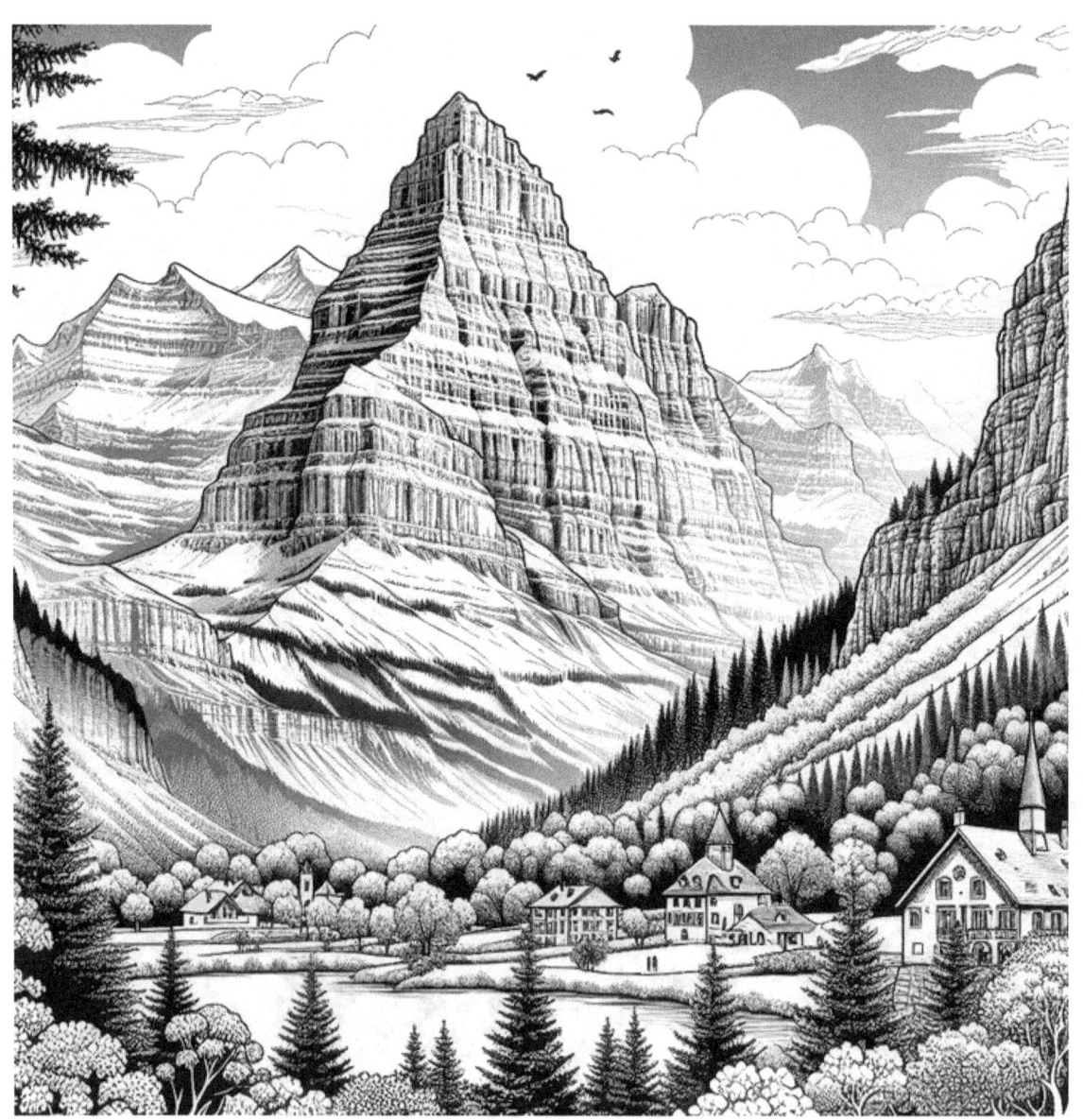

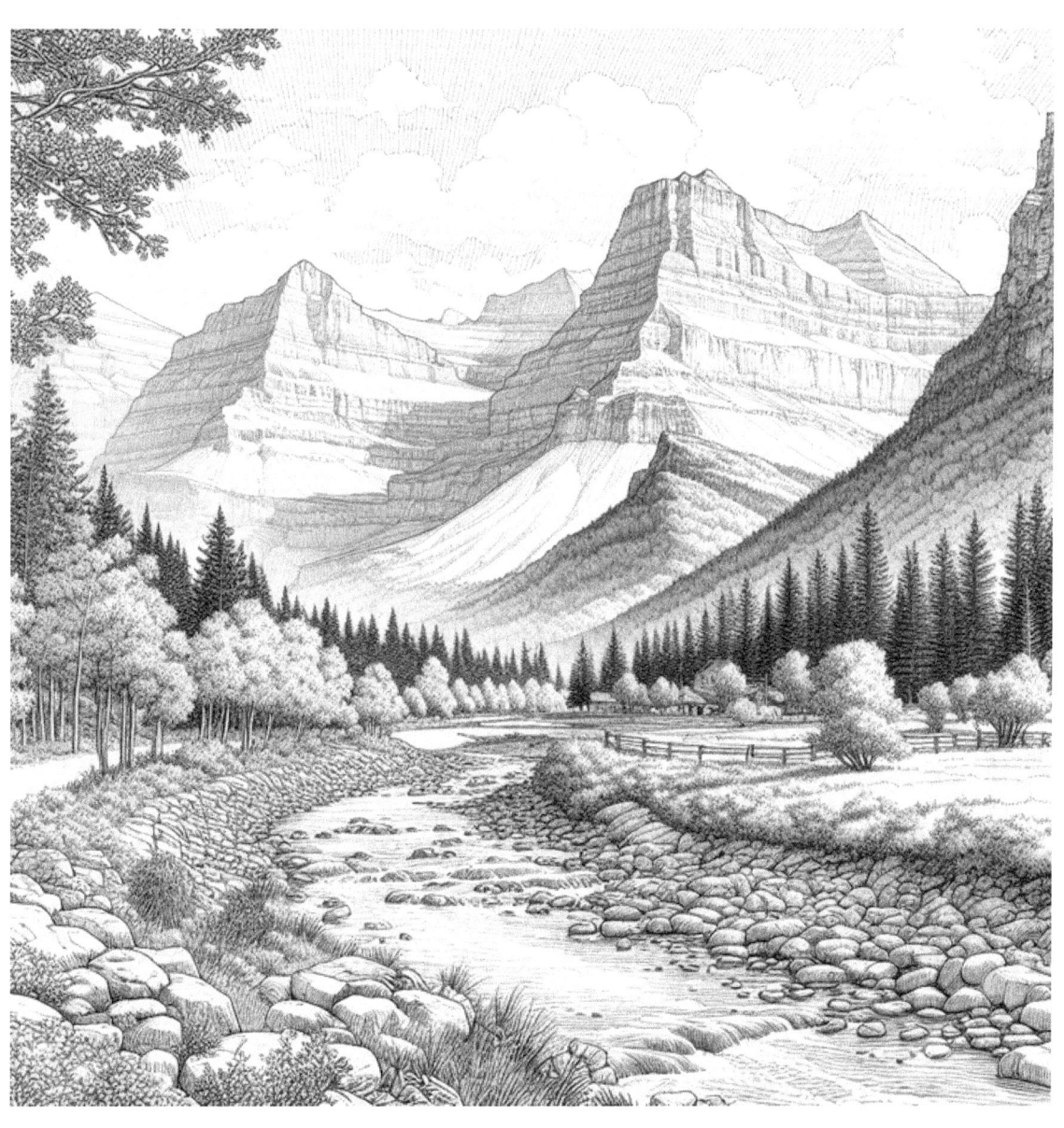

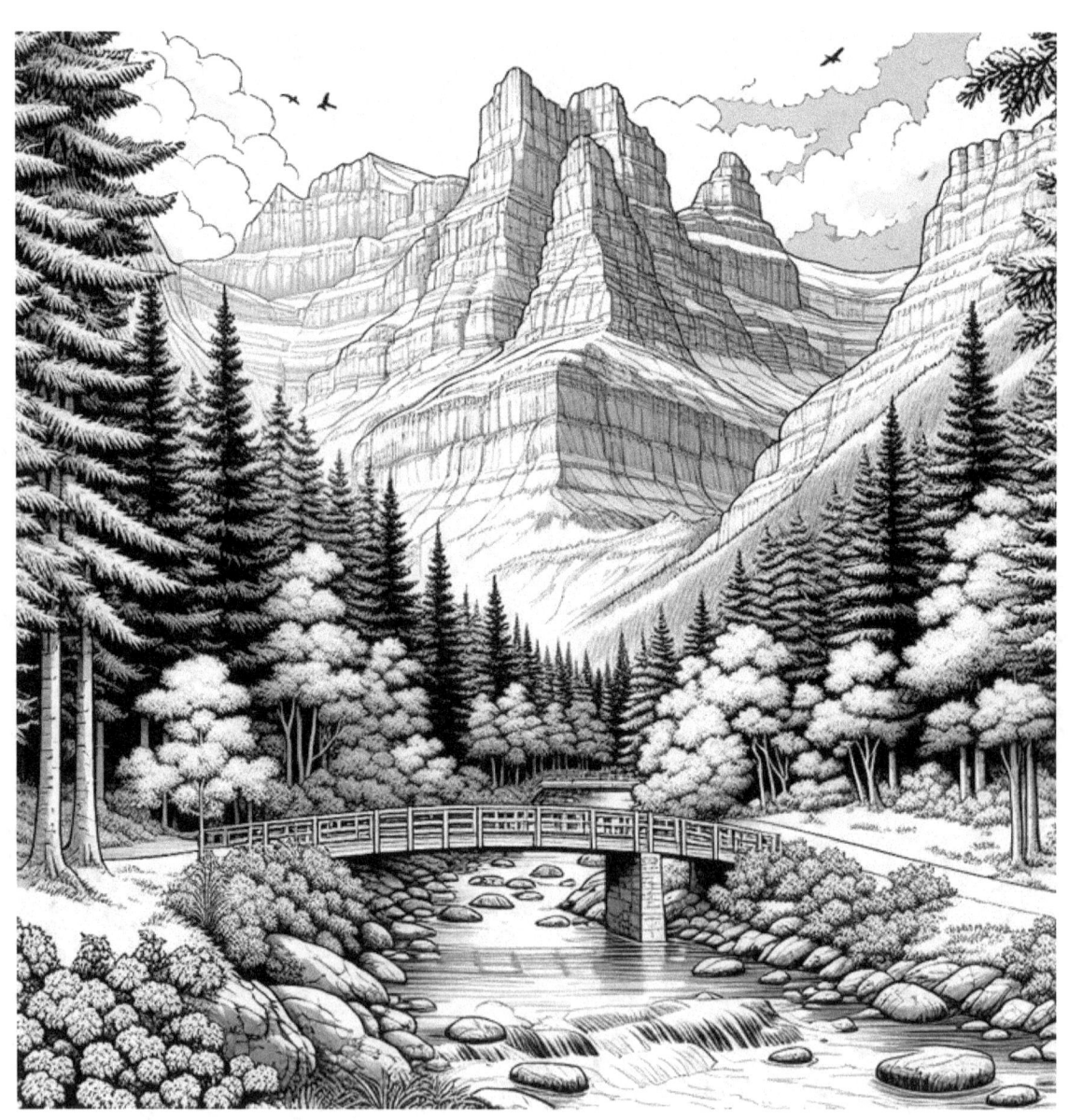

Ronda:

The New Bridge, which connects the old and new parts of the city, took over 40 years to build and is a masterpiece of 18th-century engineering.

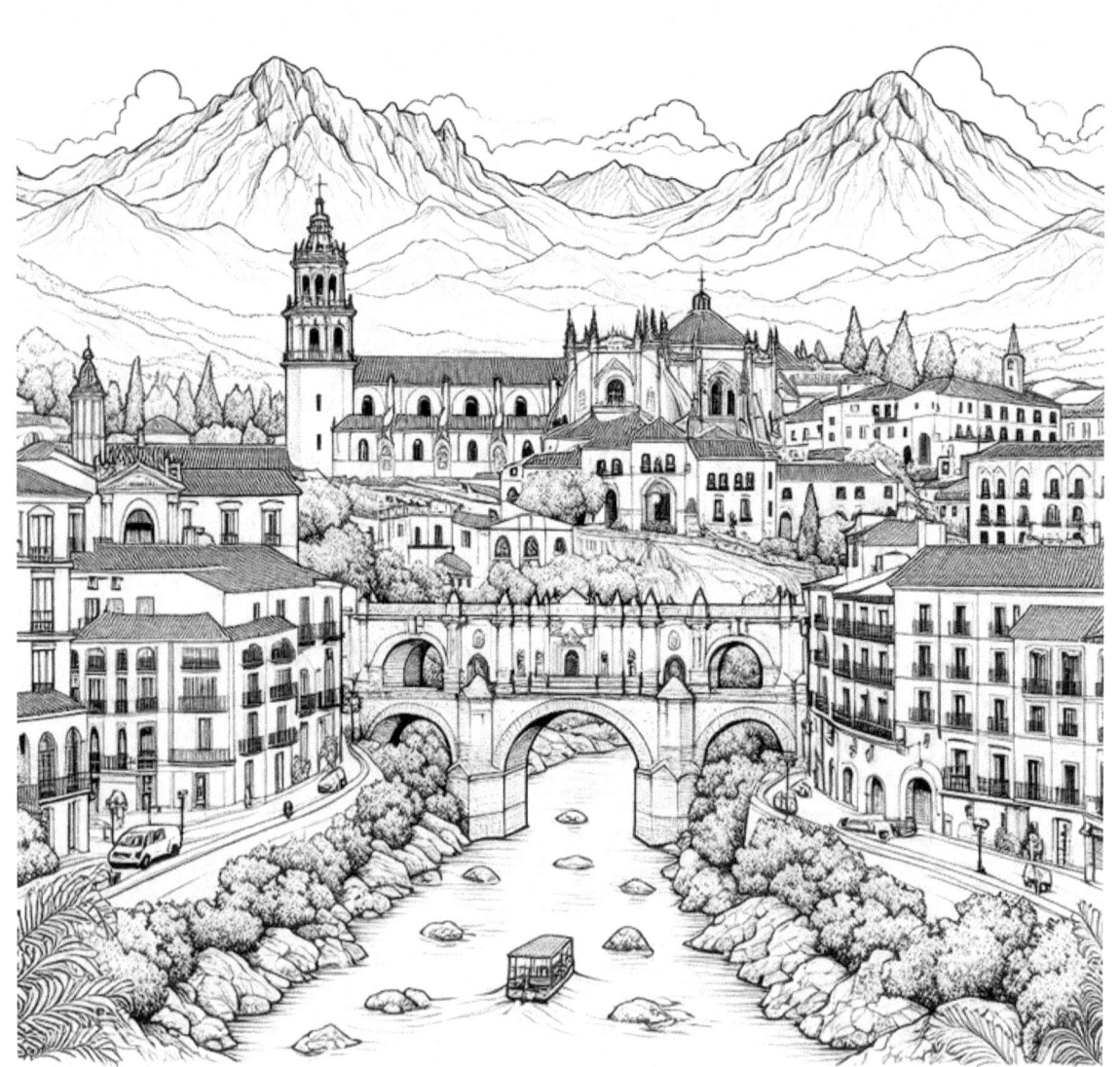

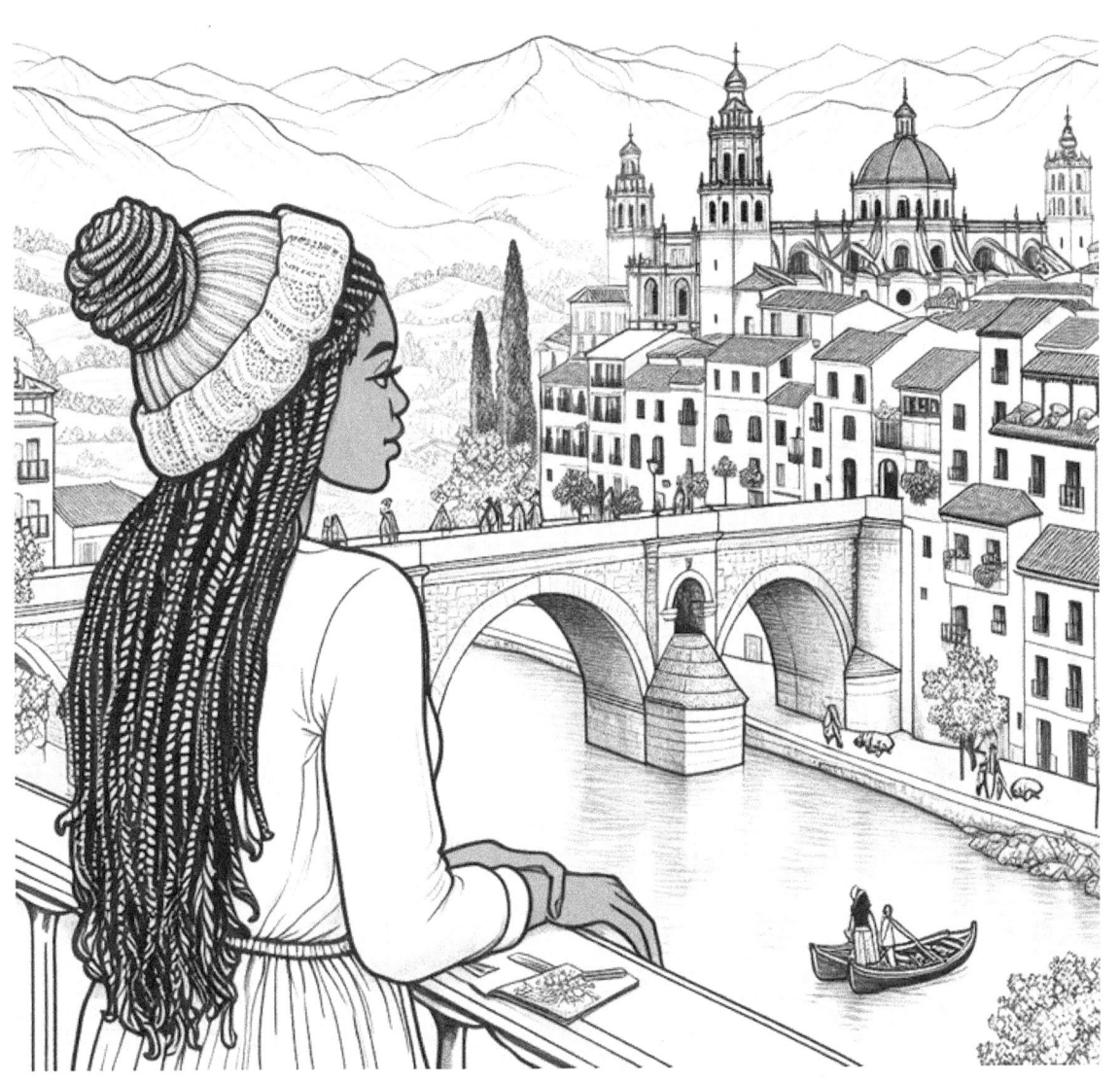

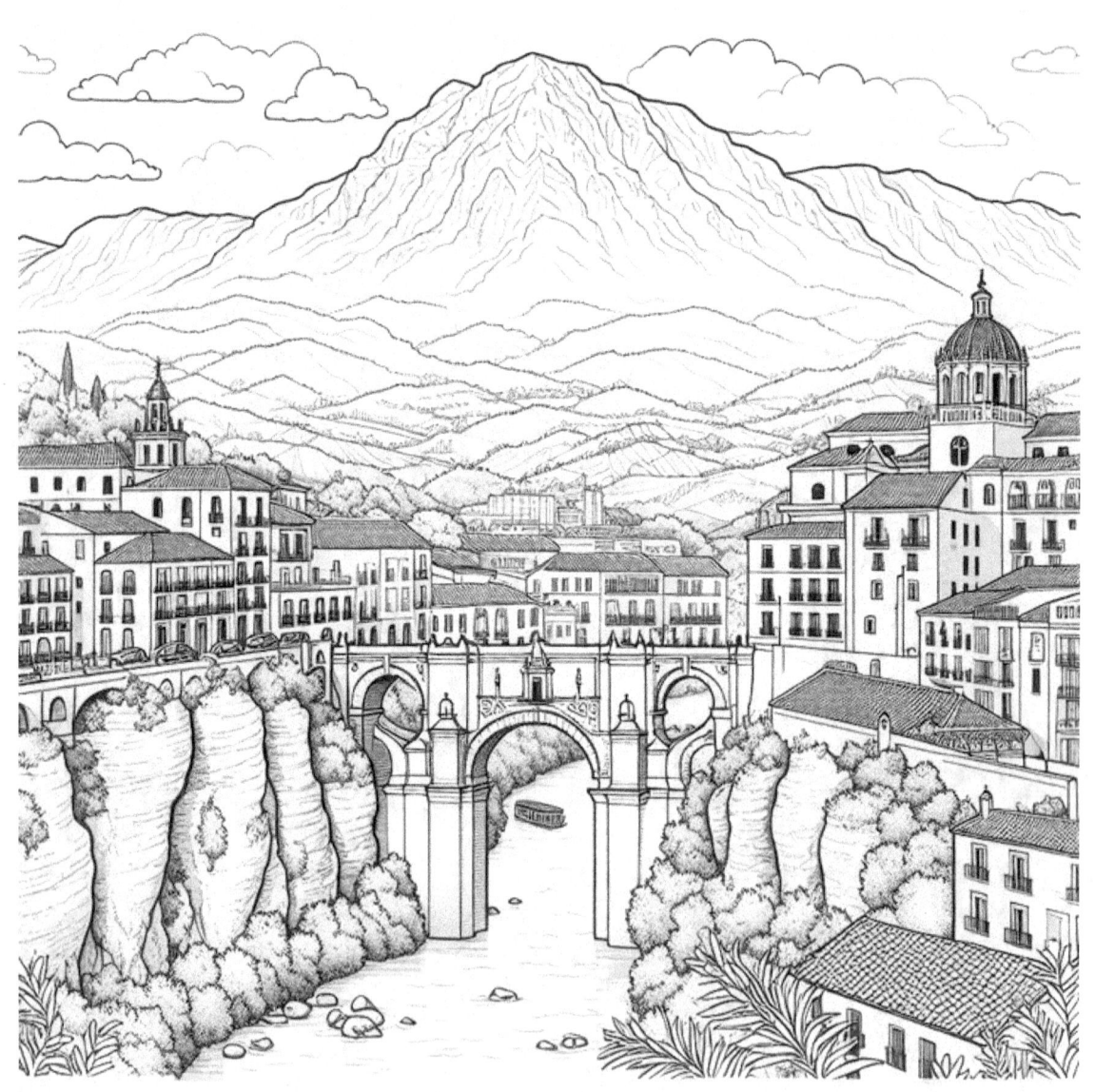

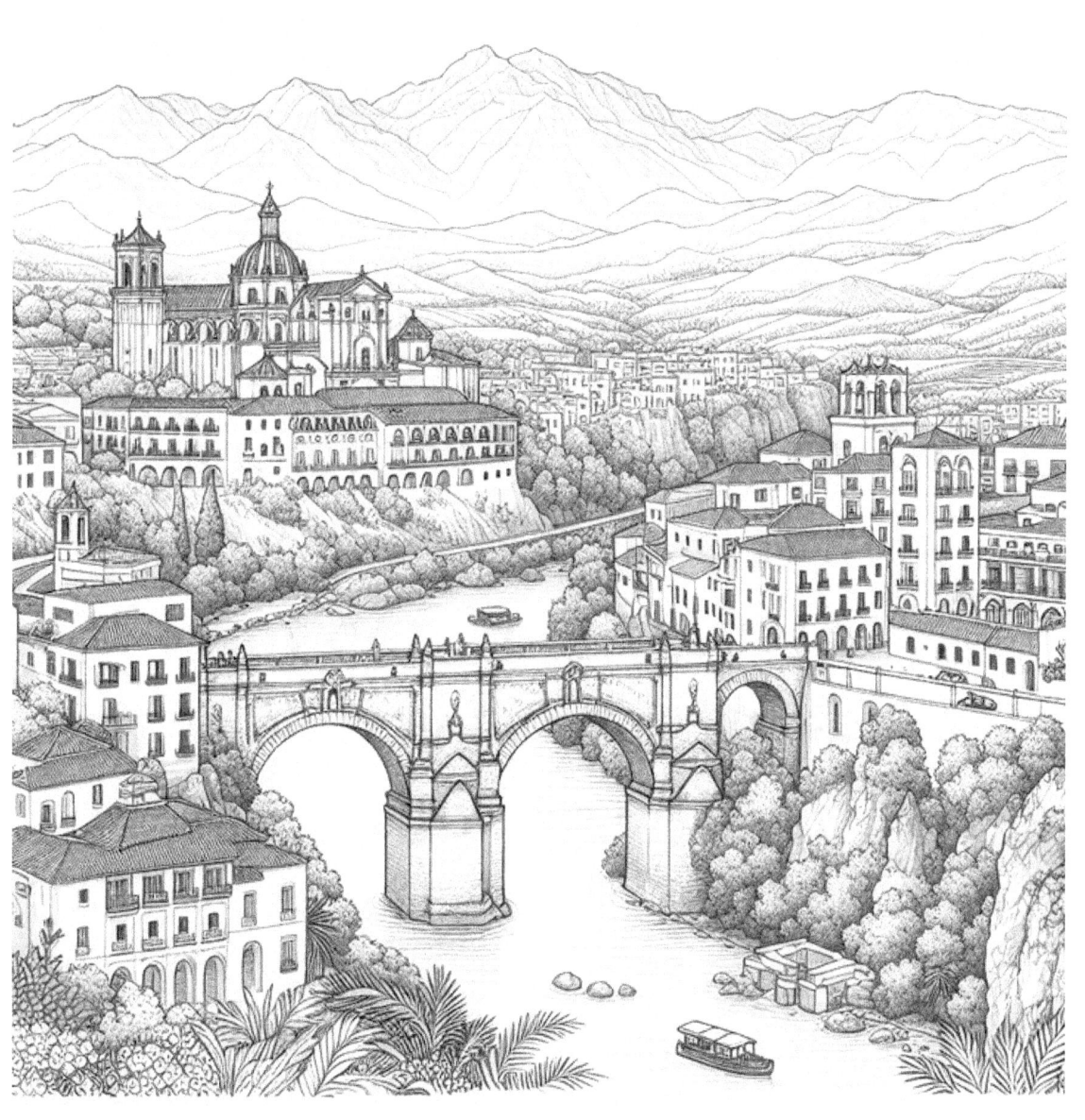

La Alhambra:

This impressive palace complex boasts over 10,000 m² of decorative tiles, known as "alicatados," adorning its walls and ceilings.

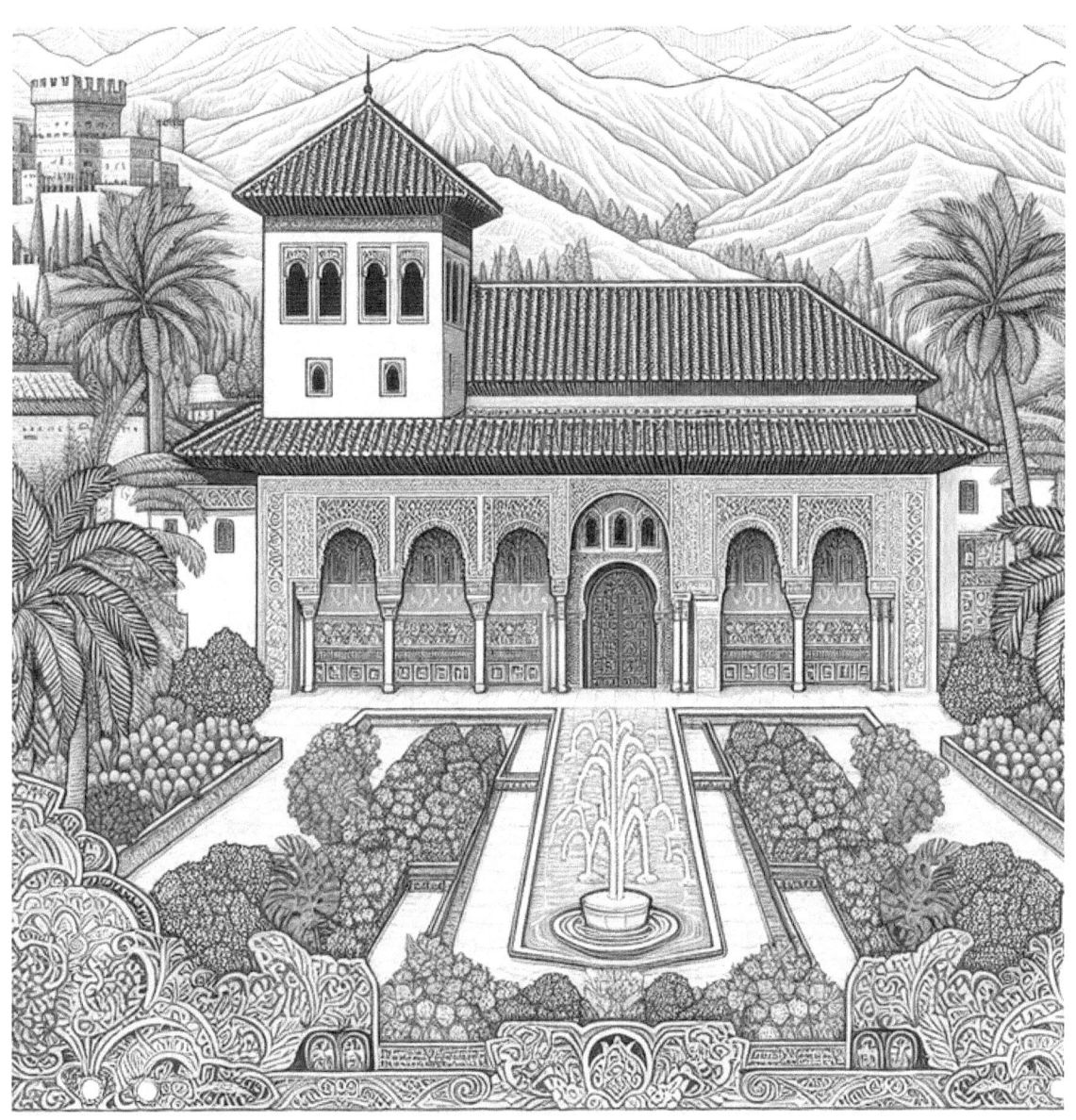

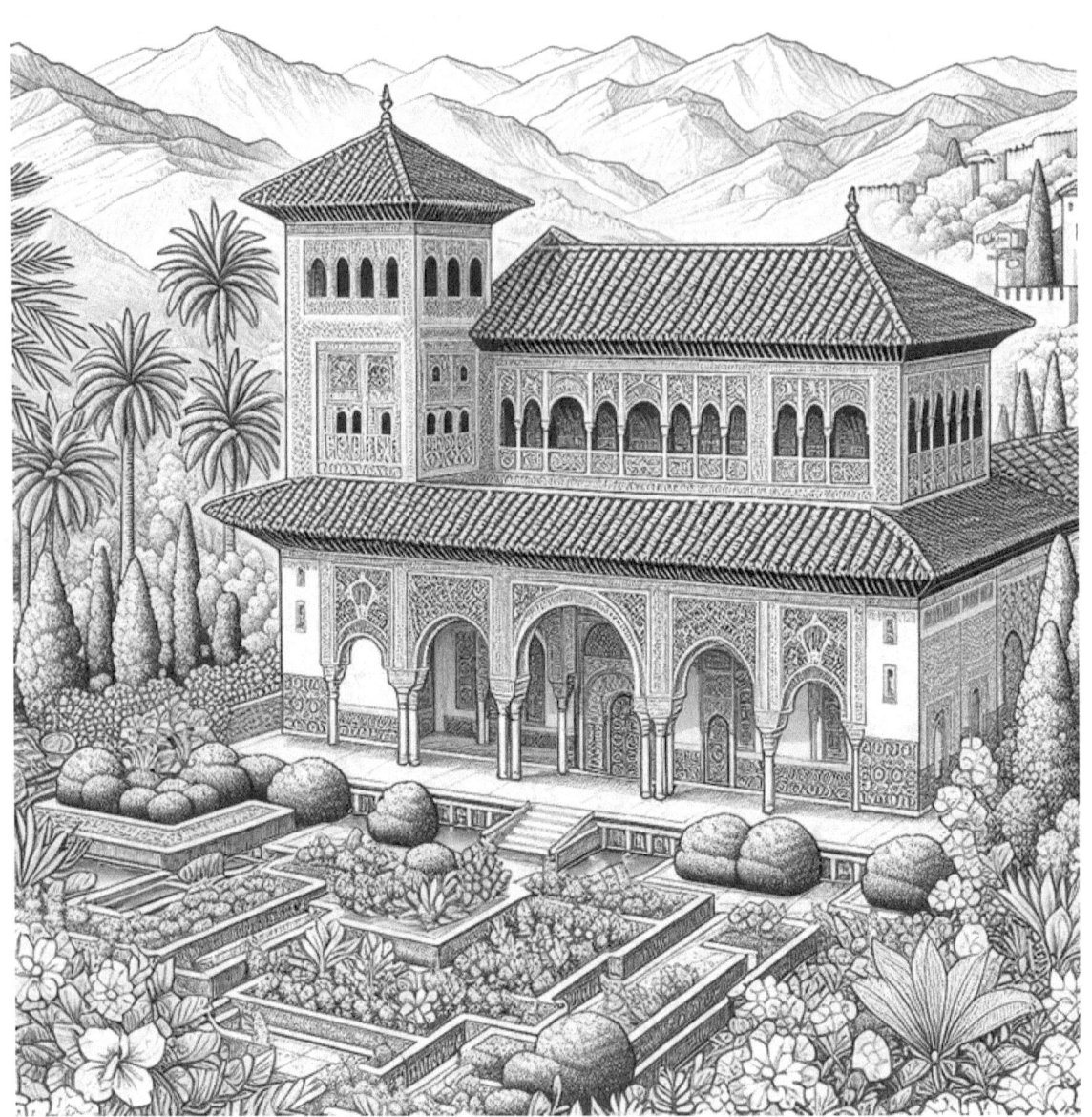

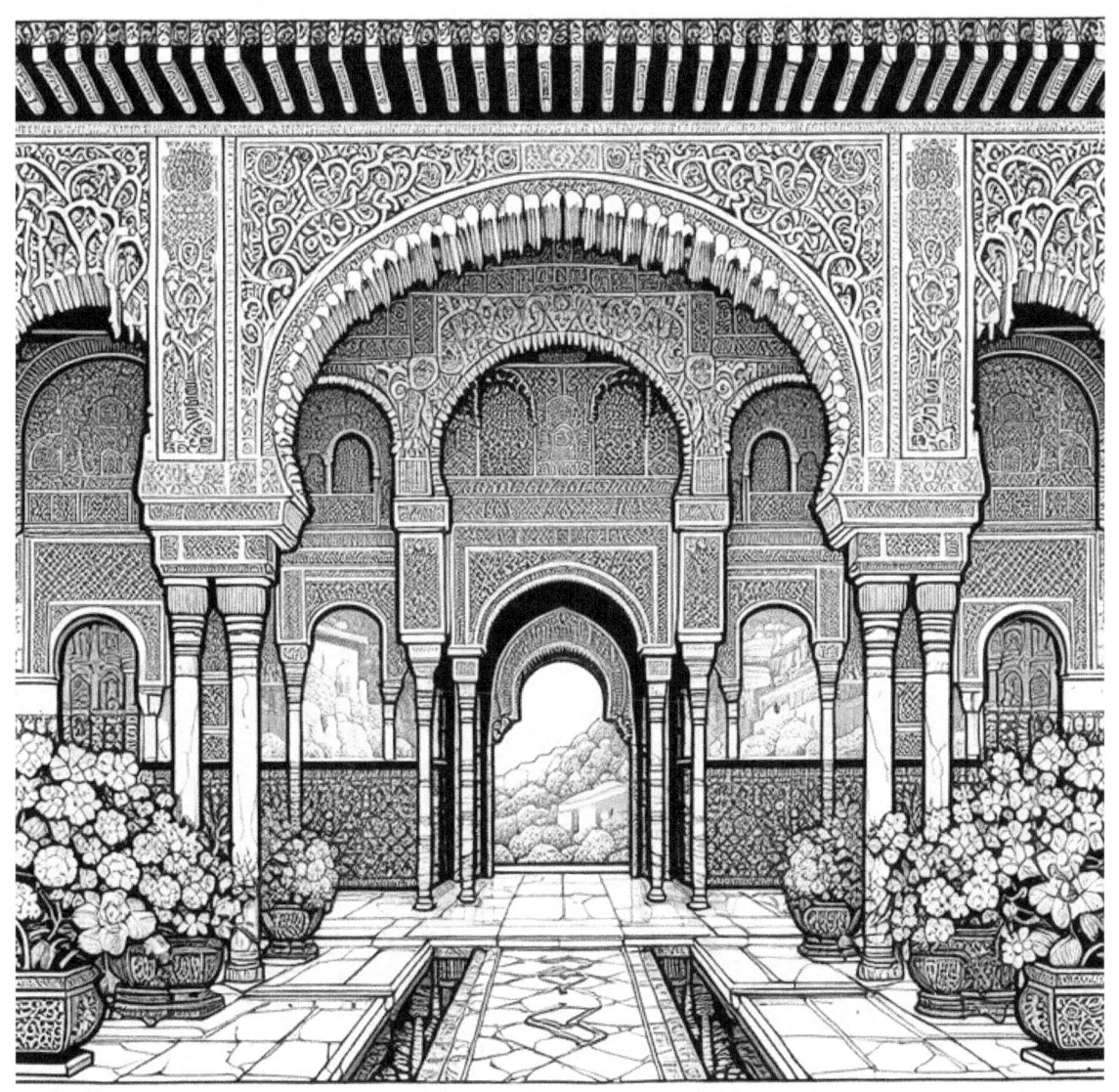

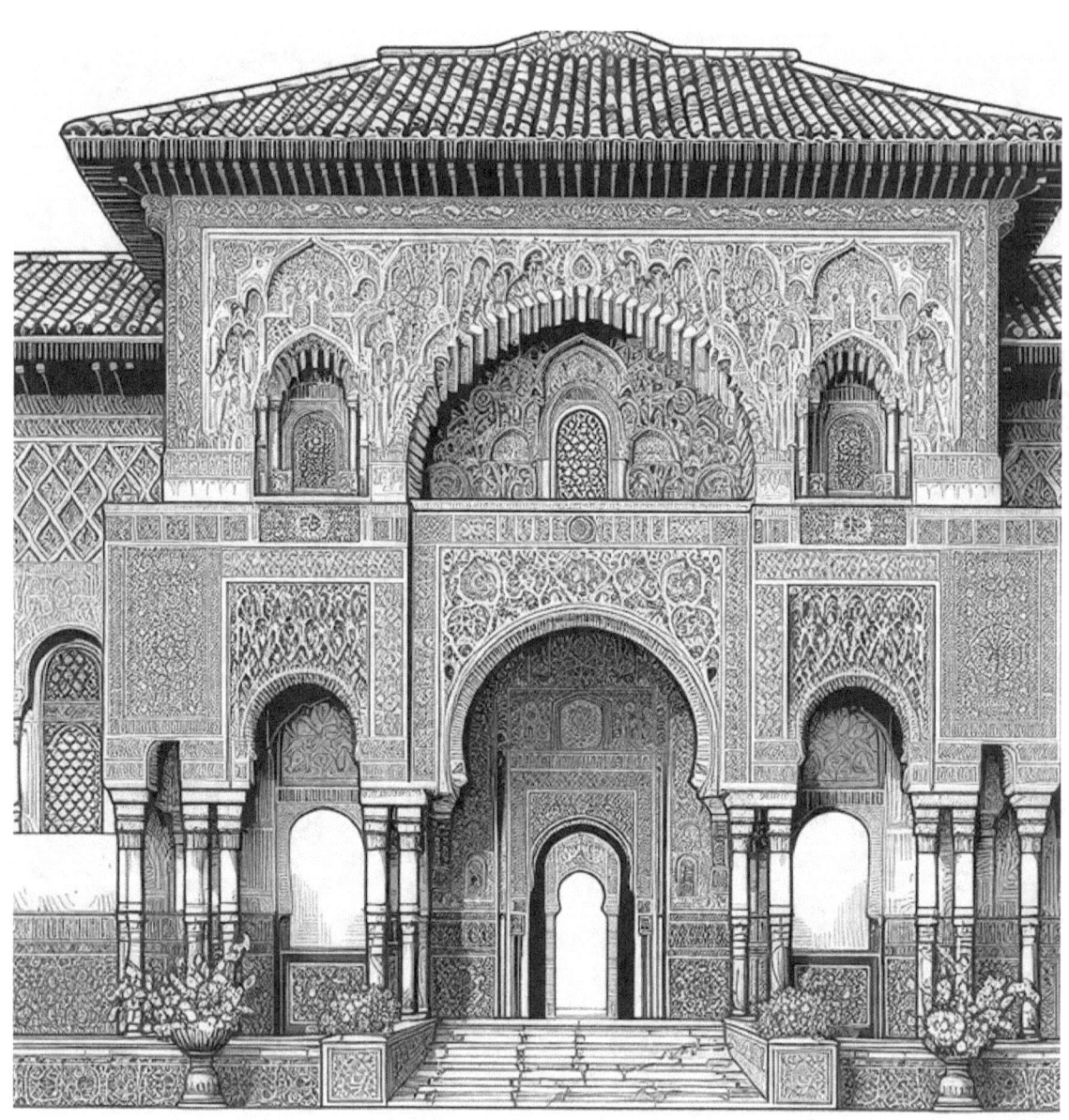

Parque Nacional de Ordesa y Monte Perdido:

In its depths lie caves and caverns that have not yet been fully explored, adding an additional mystery to its natural beauty.

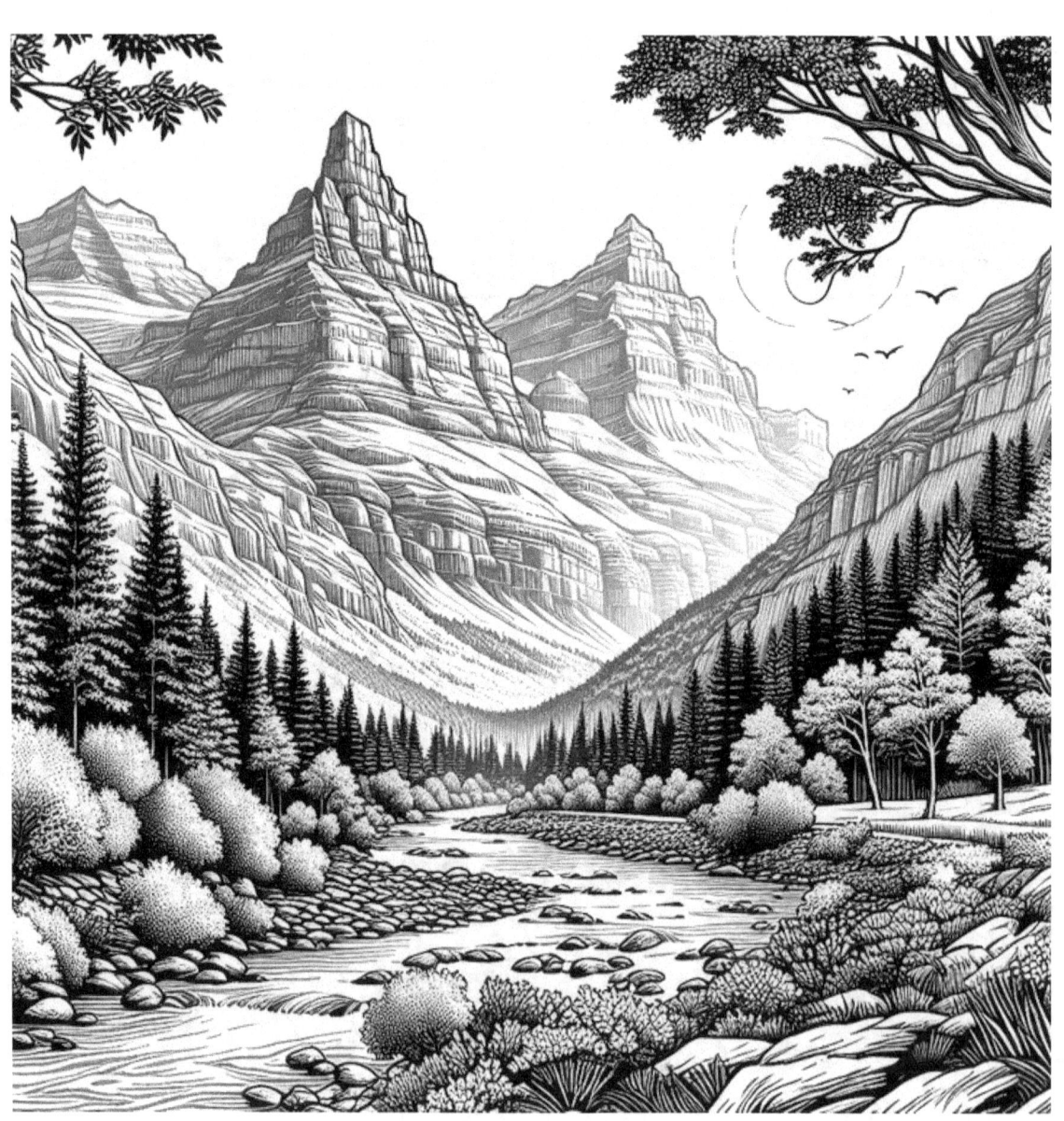

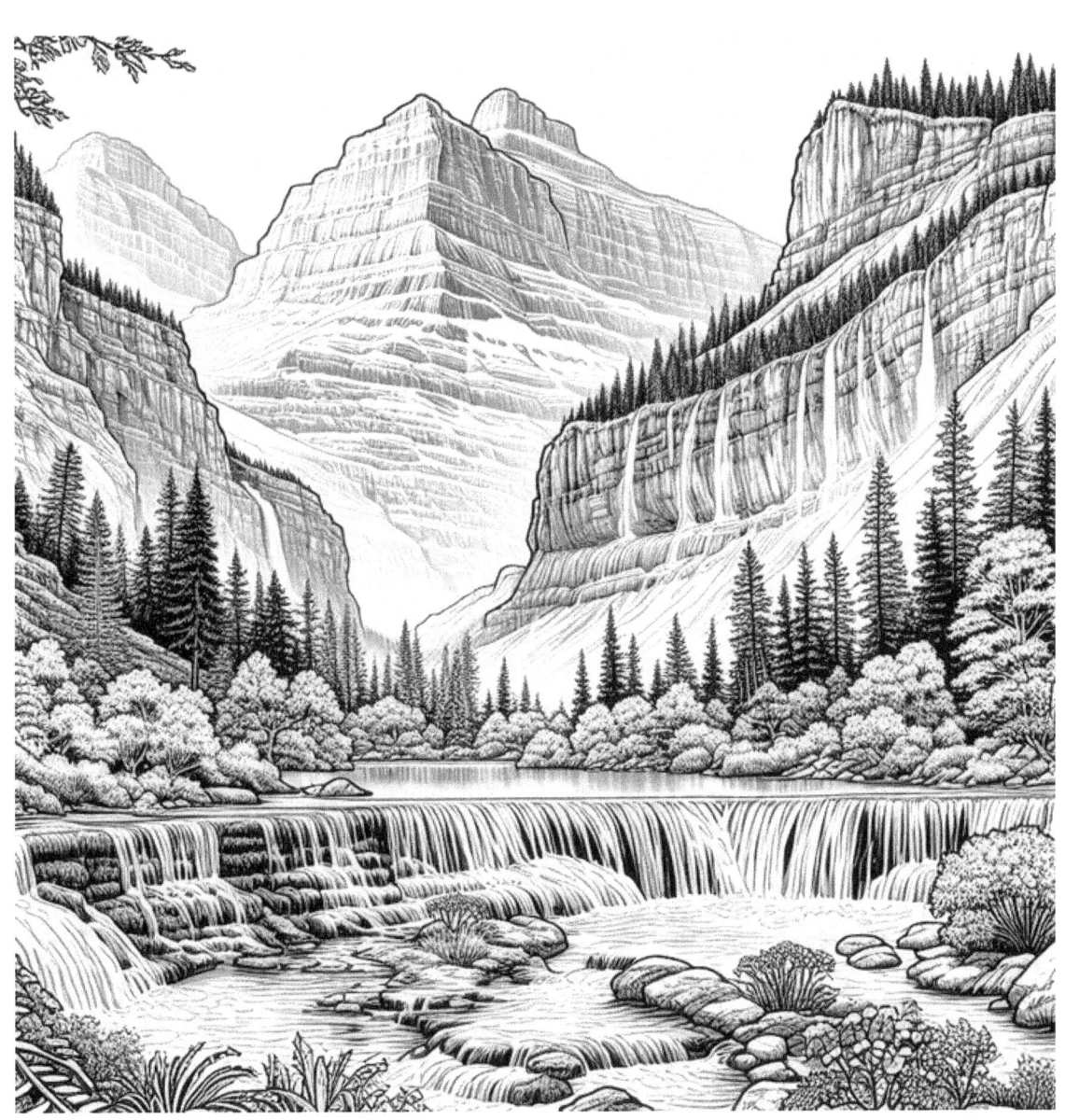

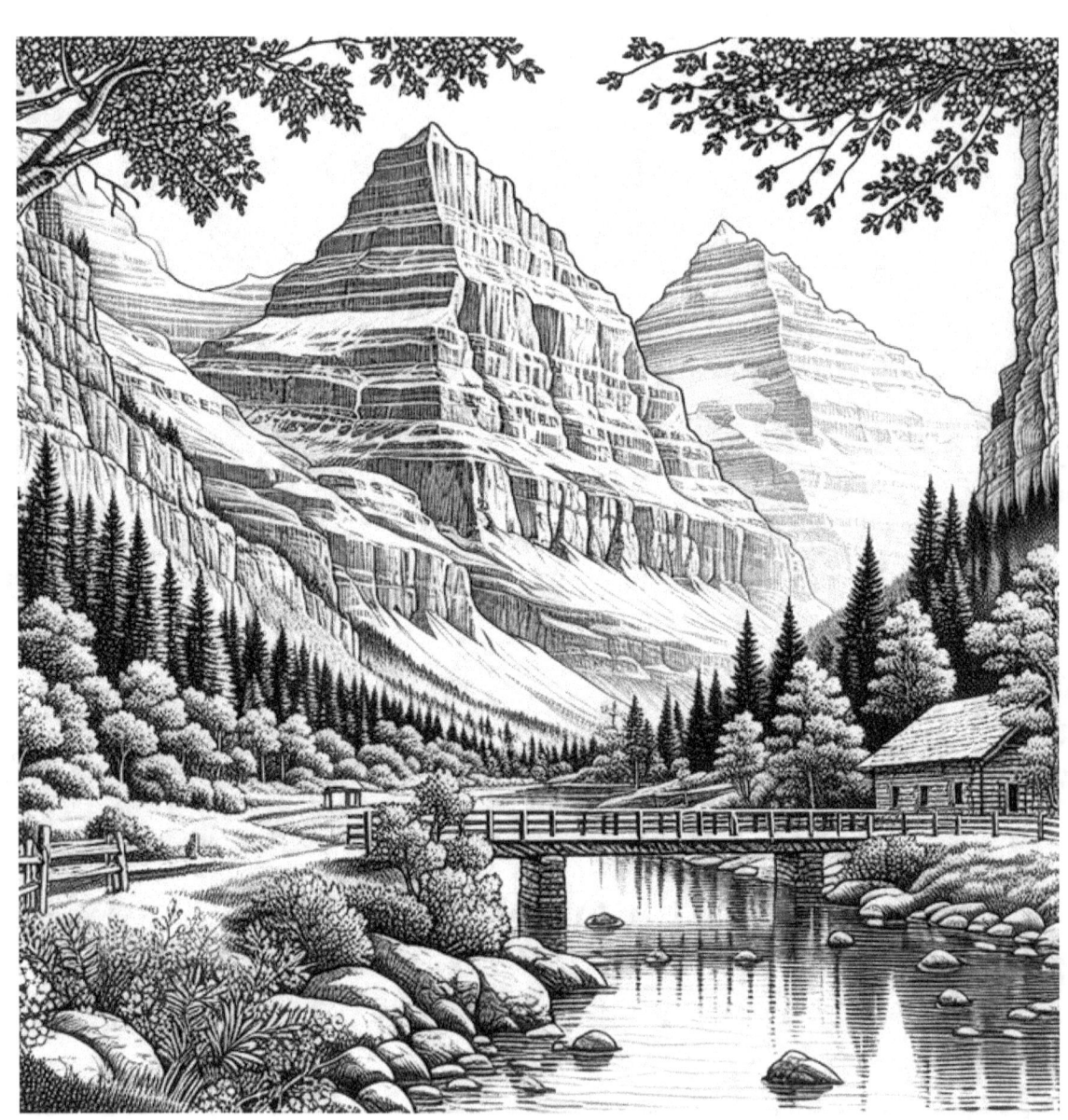

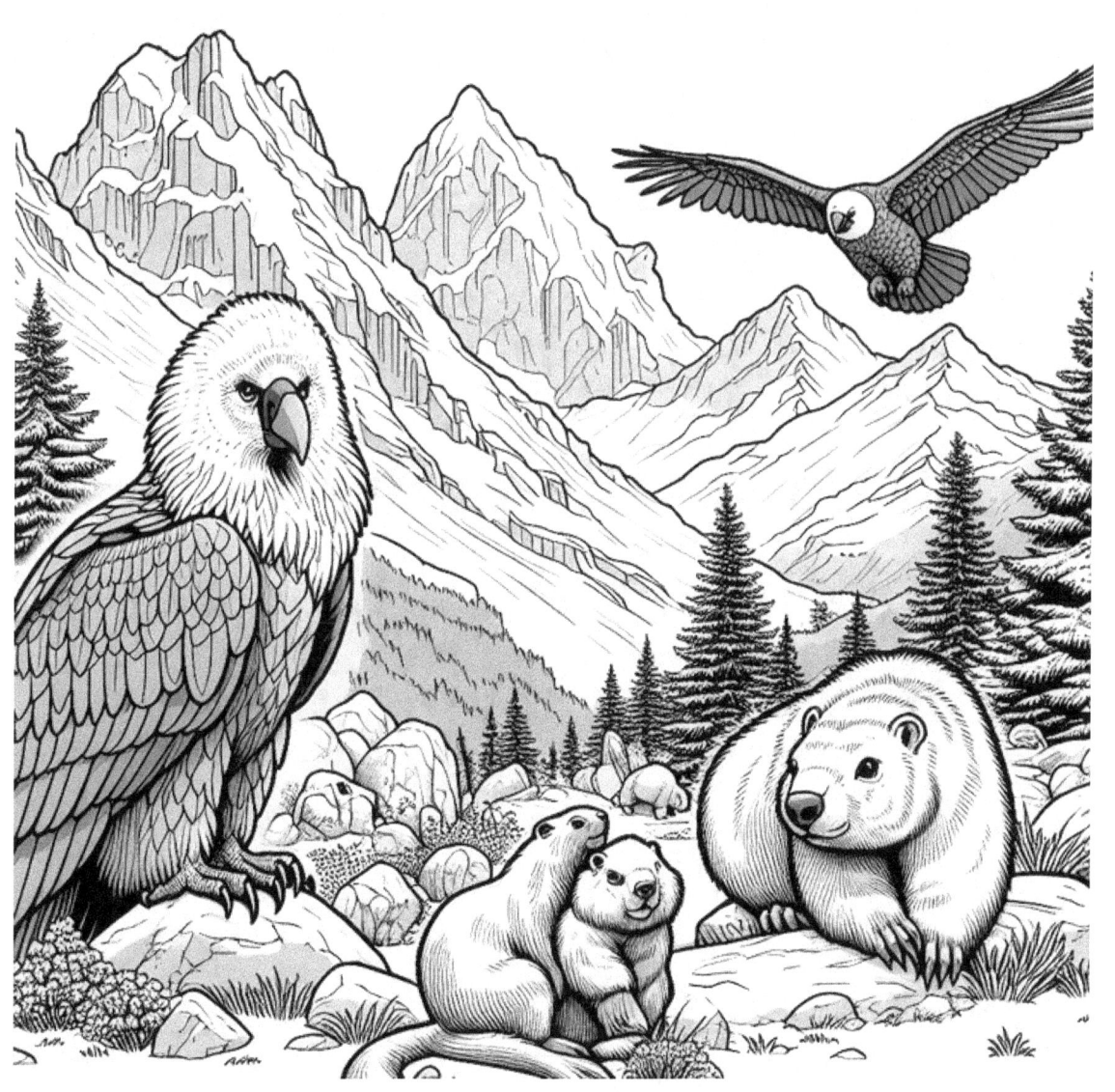

Las Islas Cíes:

During the Roman era, these islands were known as the "islands of the gods," and it was believed that they were inhabited by divine beings.

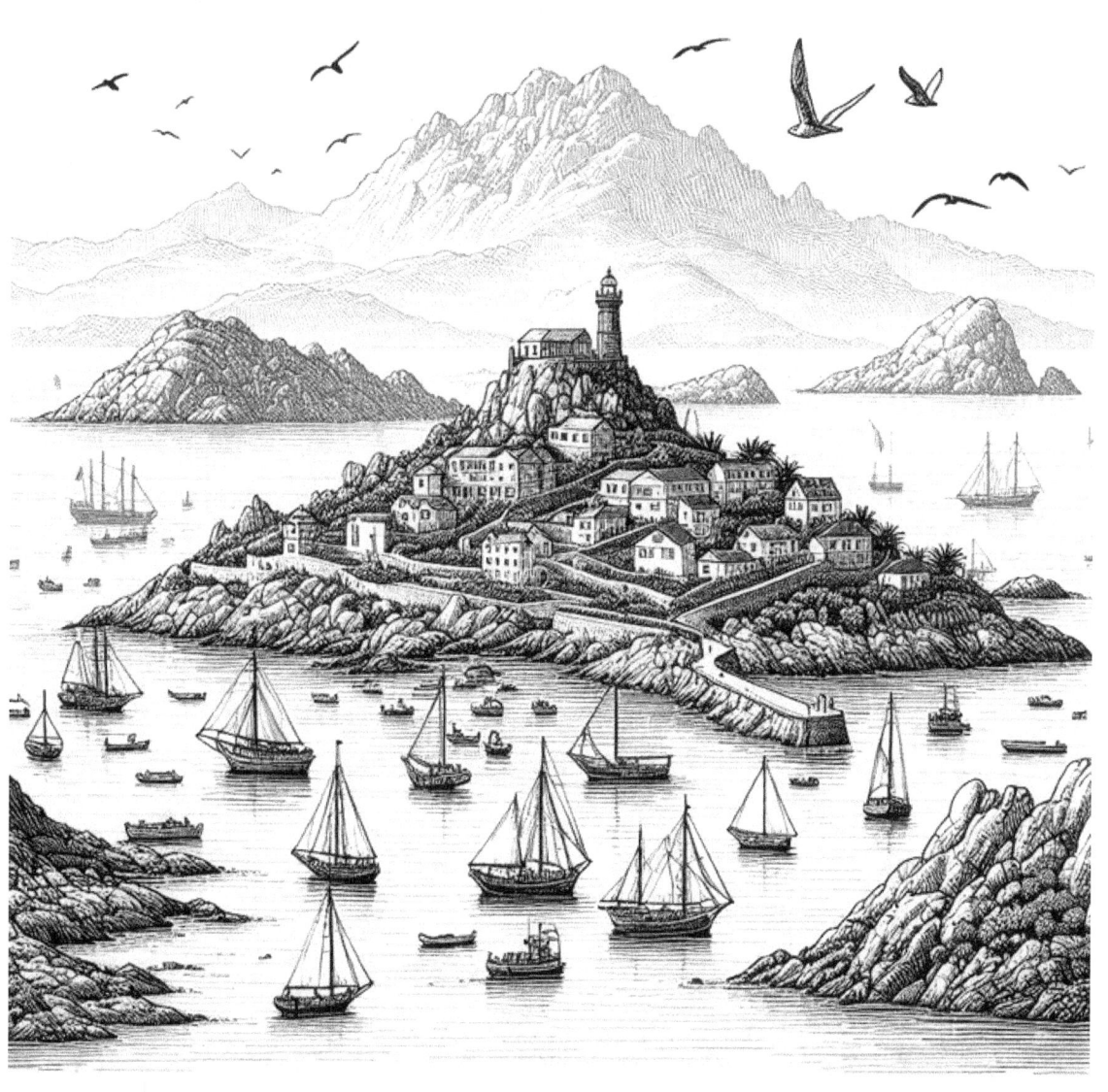

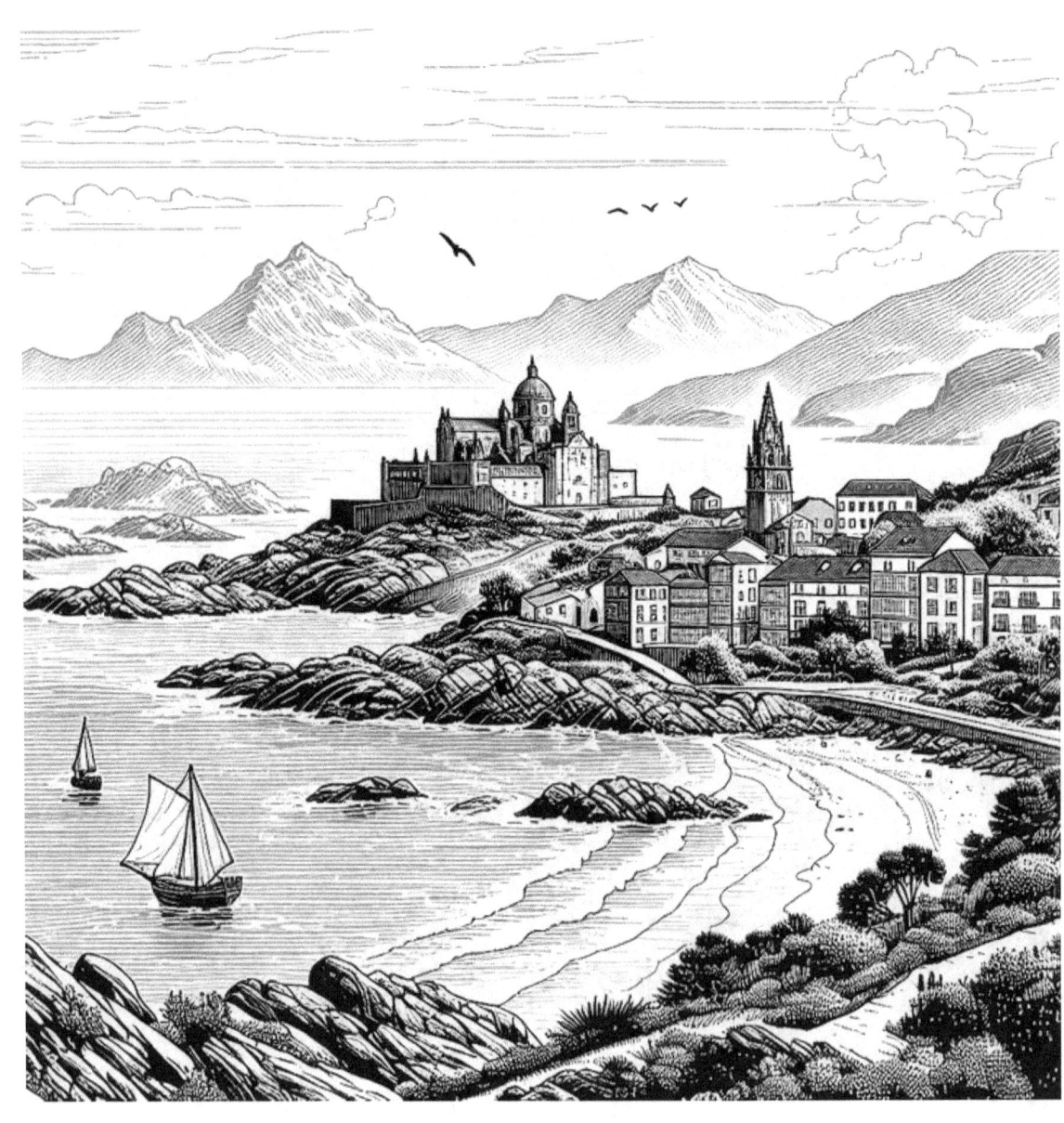

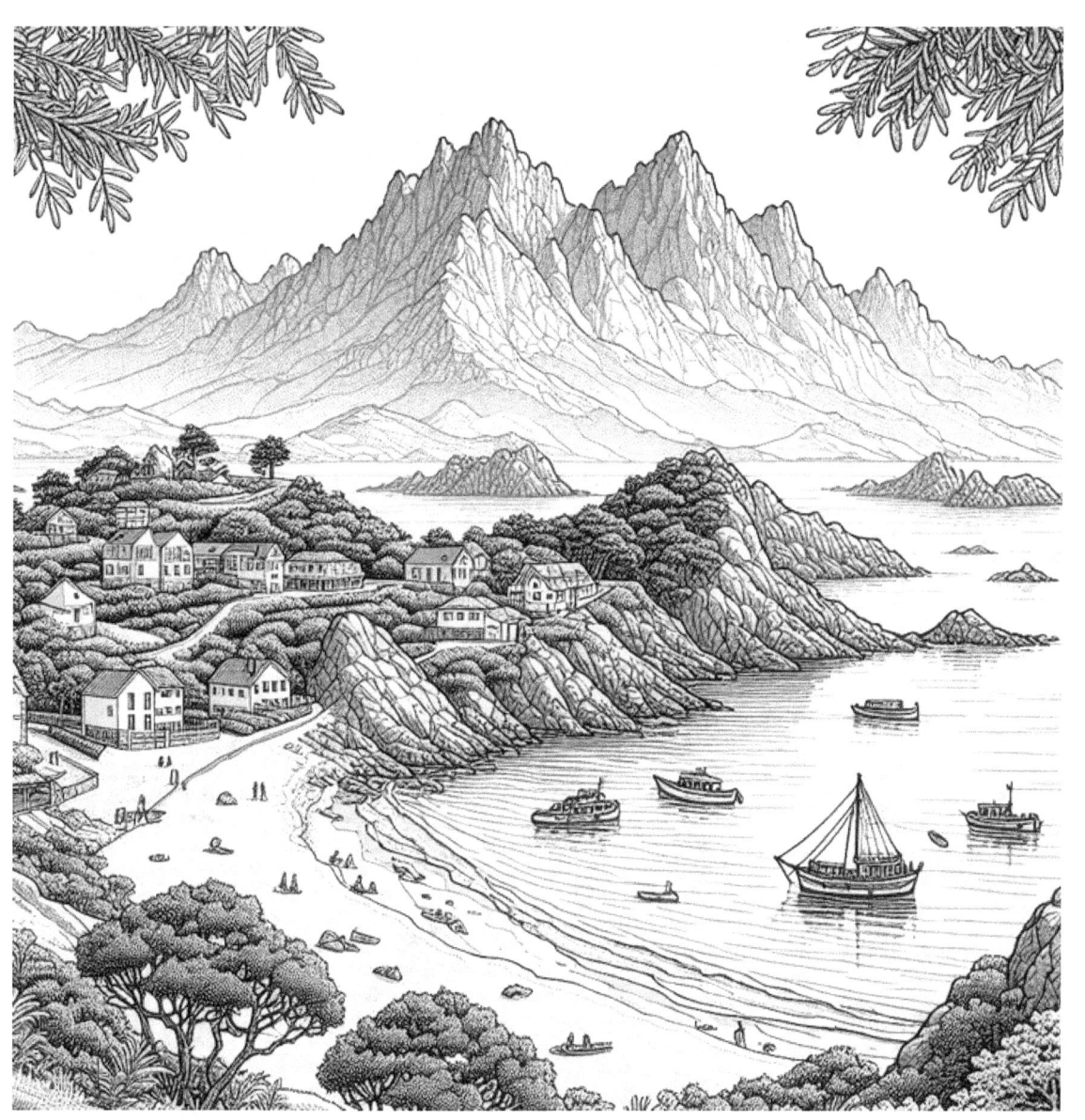

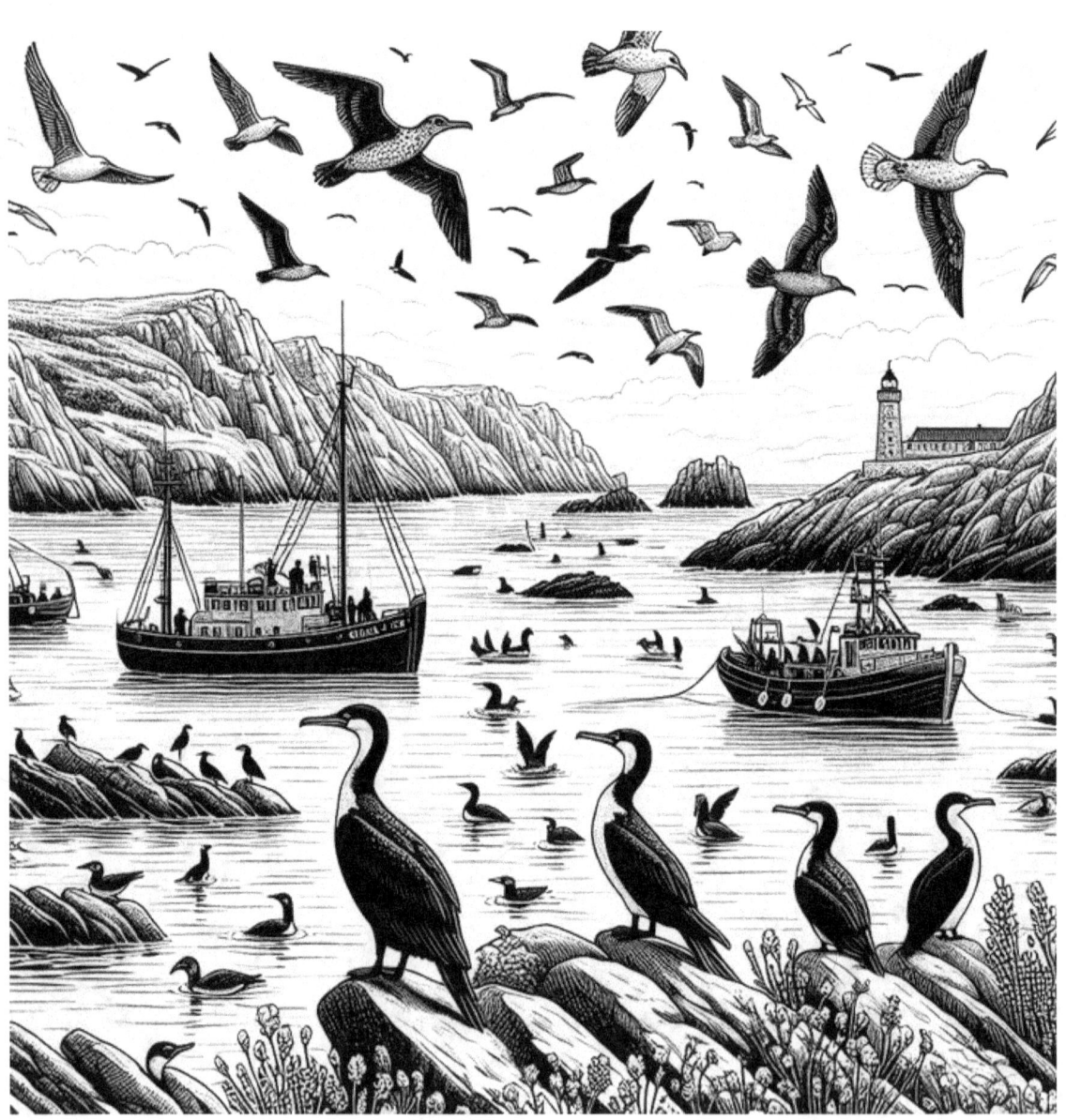

Cañón del Sil:

On the slopes of this canyon, vineyards are cultivated in terraces known for producing wines of excellent quality, thanks to the influence of the climate and soil.

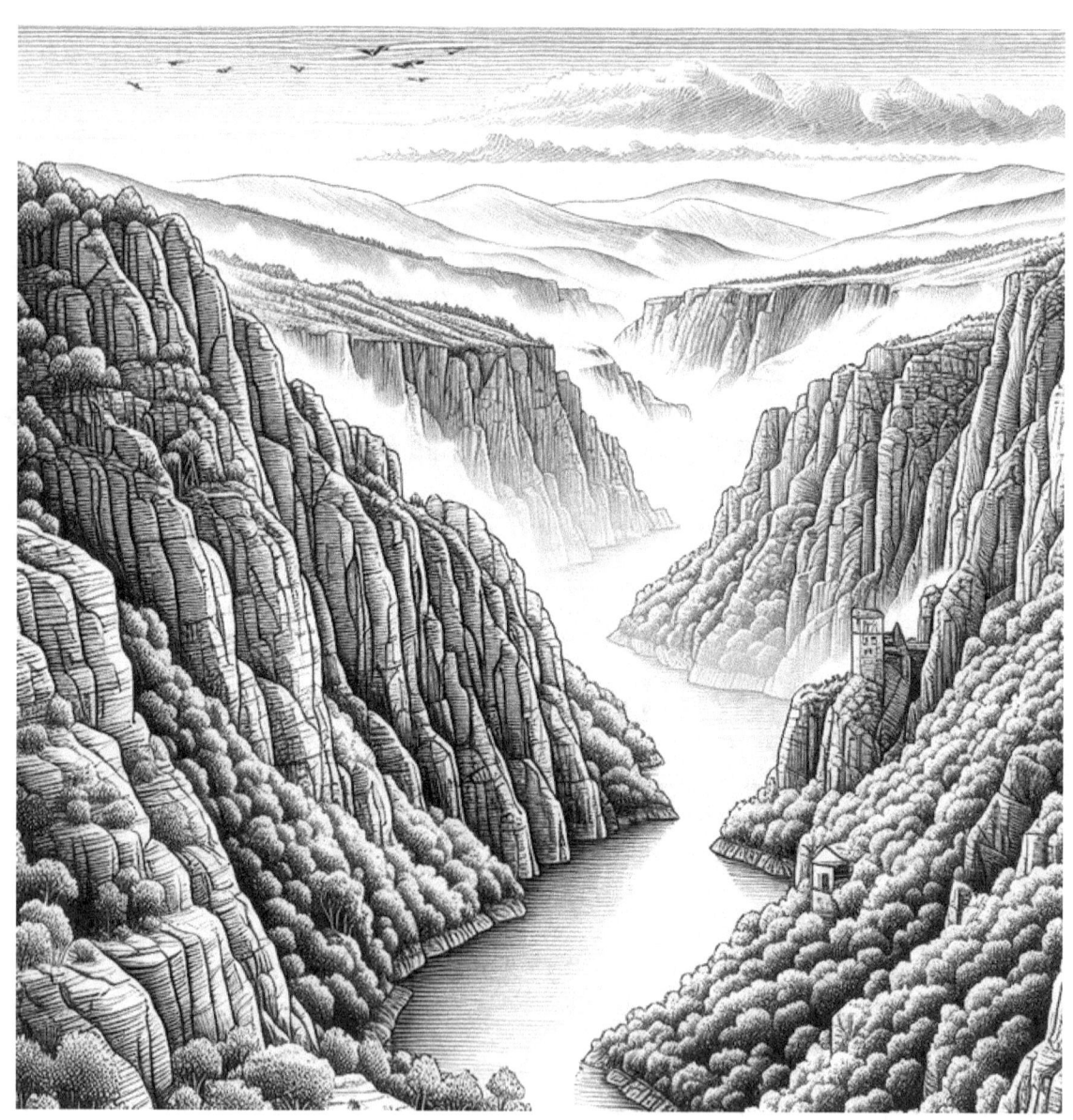

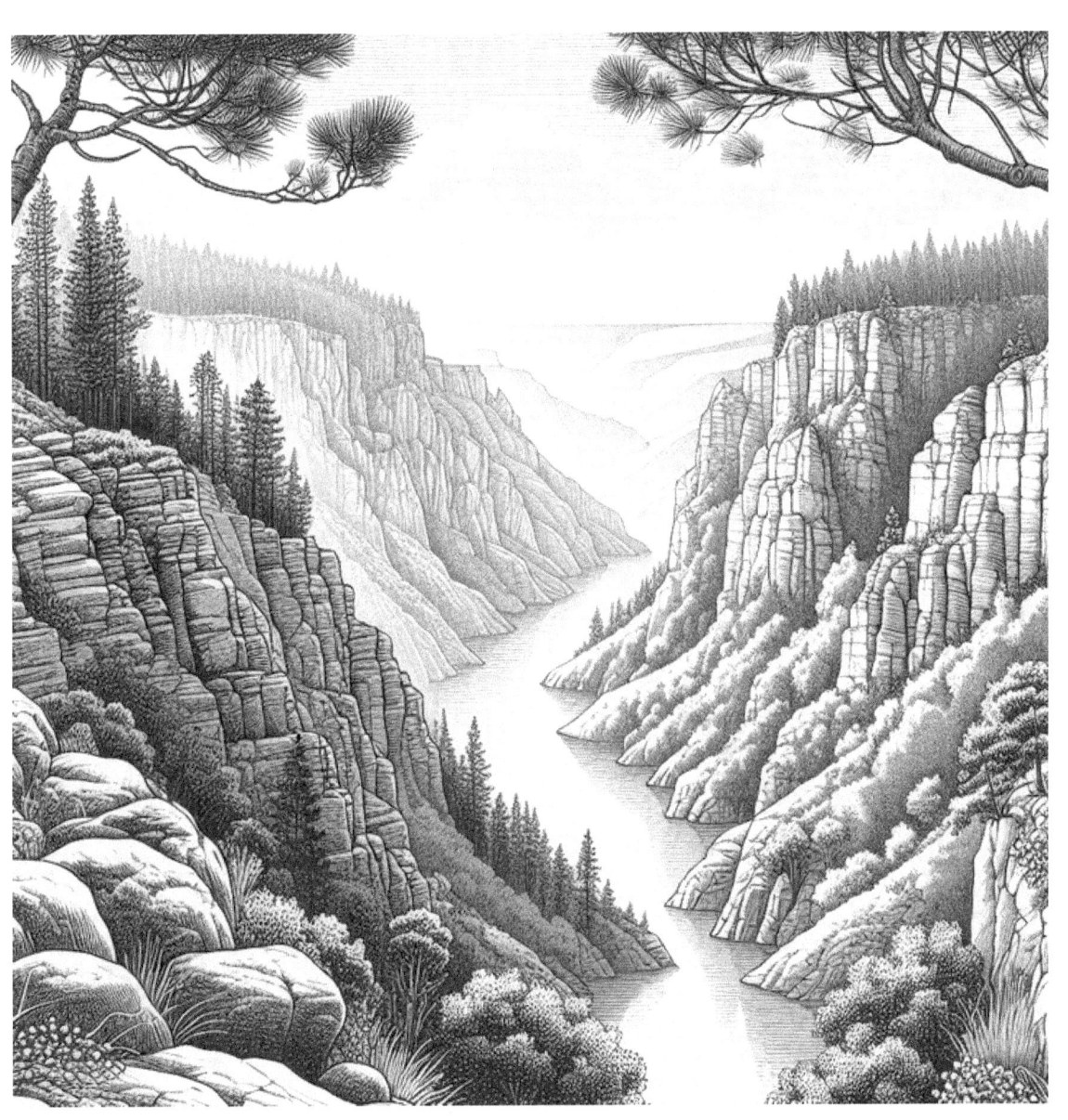

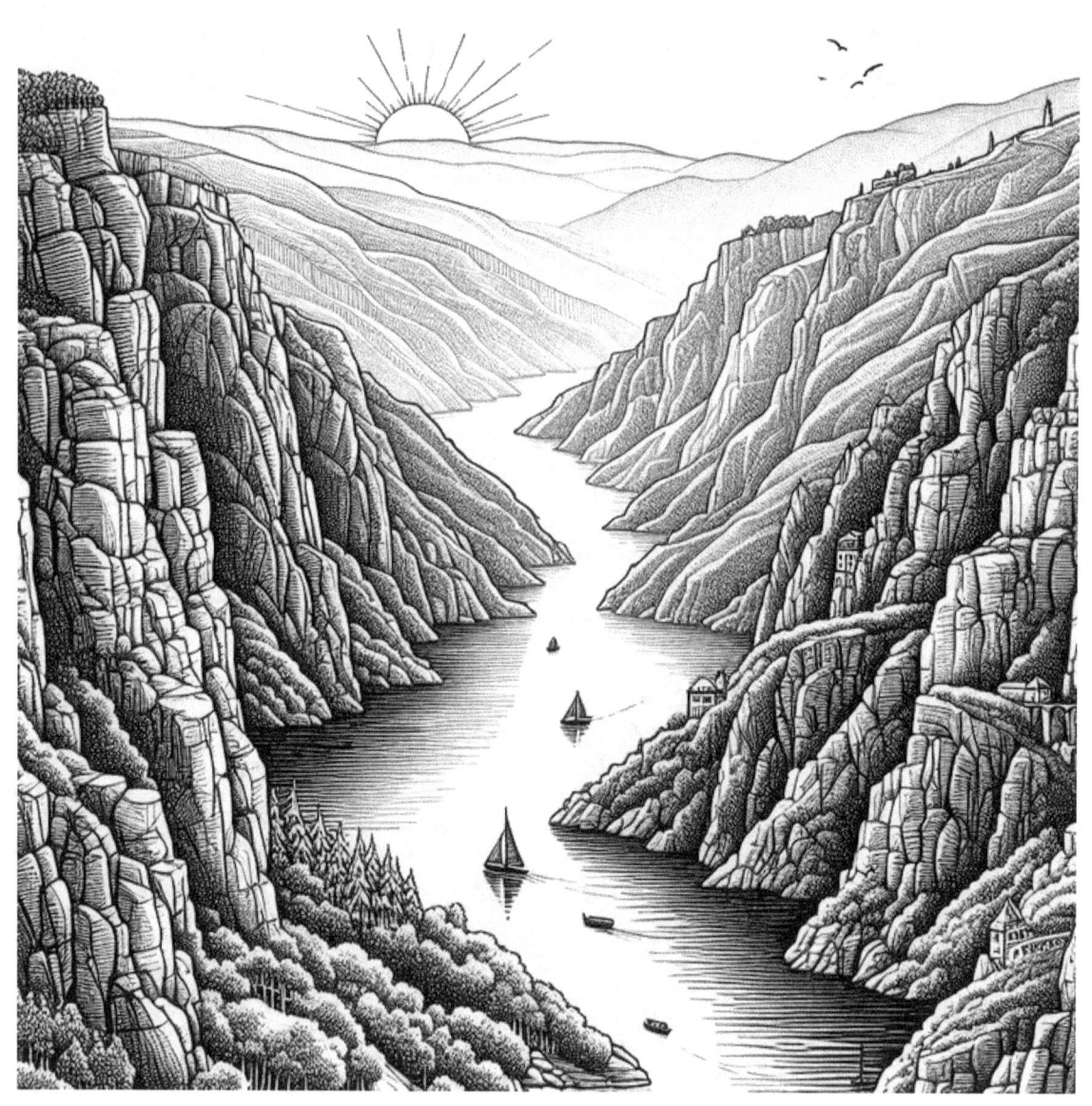

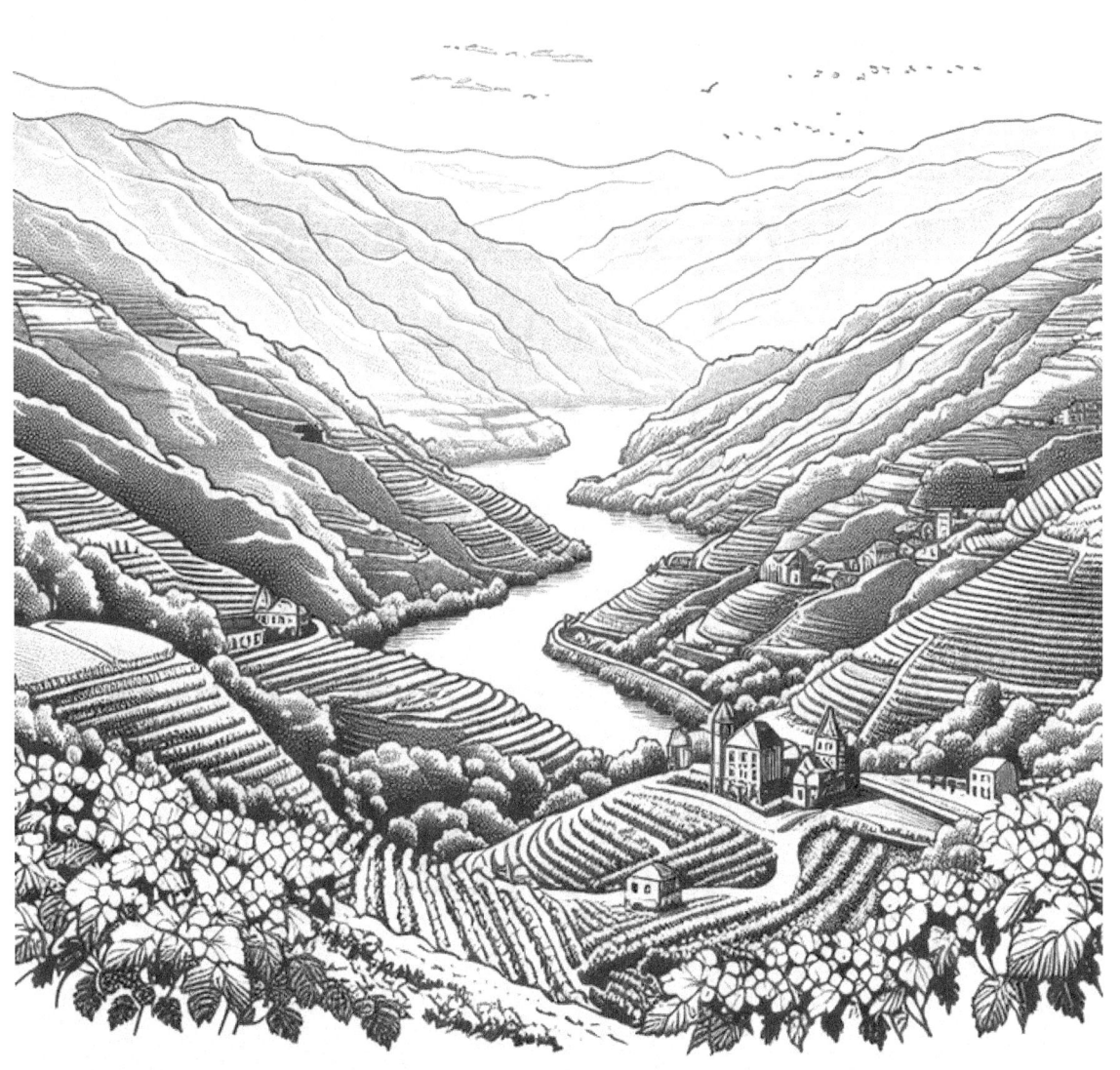

Parque Nacional de Garajonay:

It is one of the few places in the world where the laurisilva, a type of subtropical forest that existed in the Tertiary era, is still preserved.

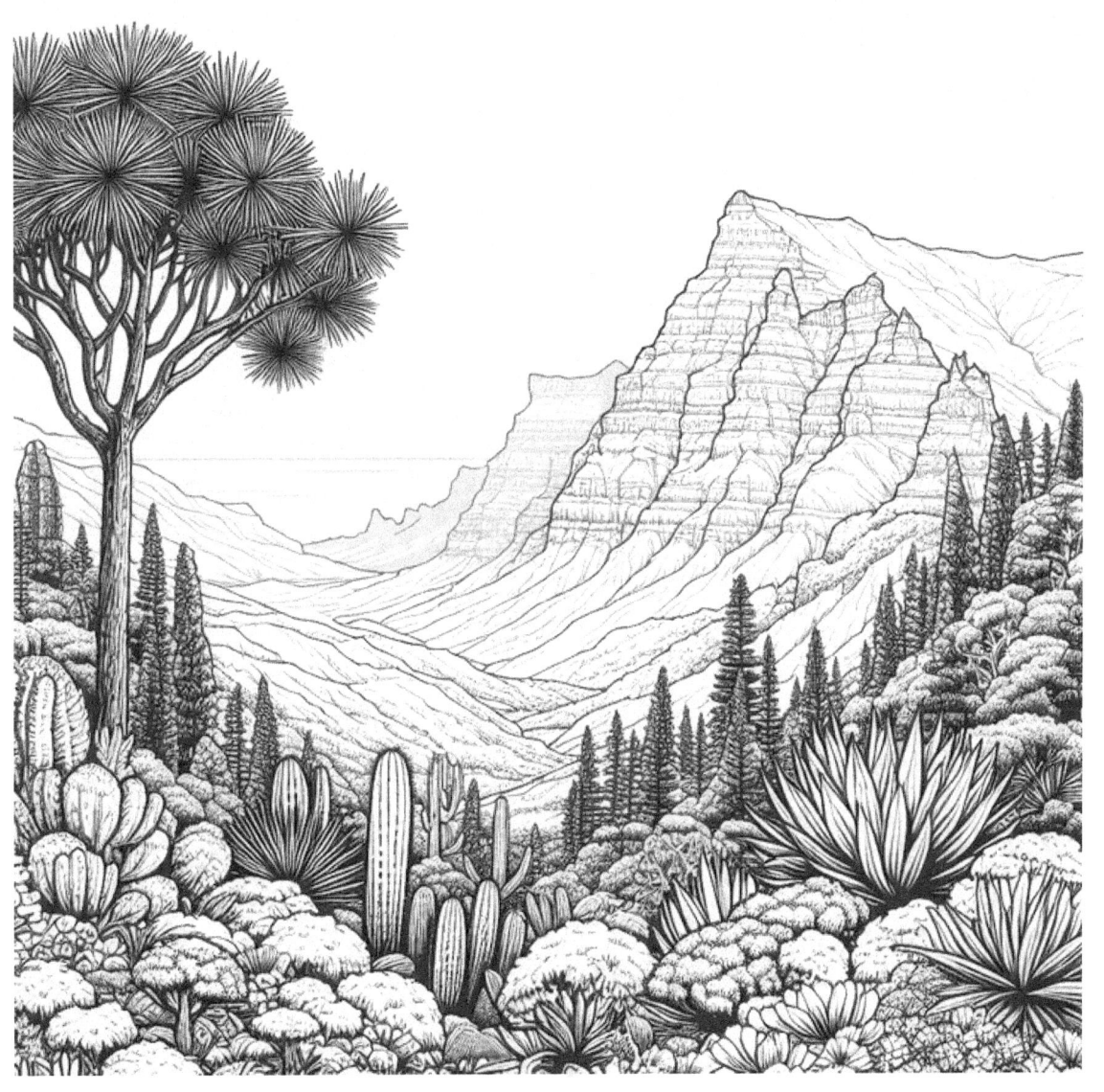

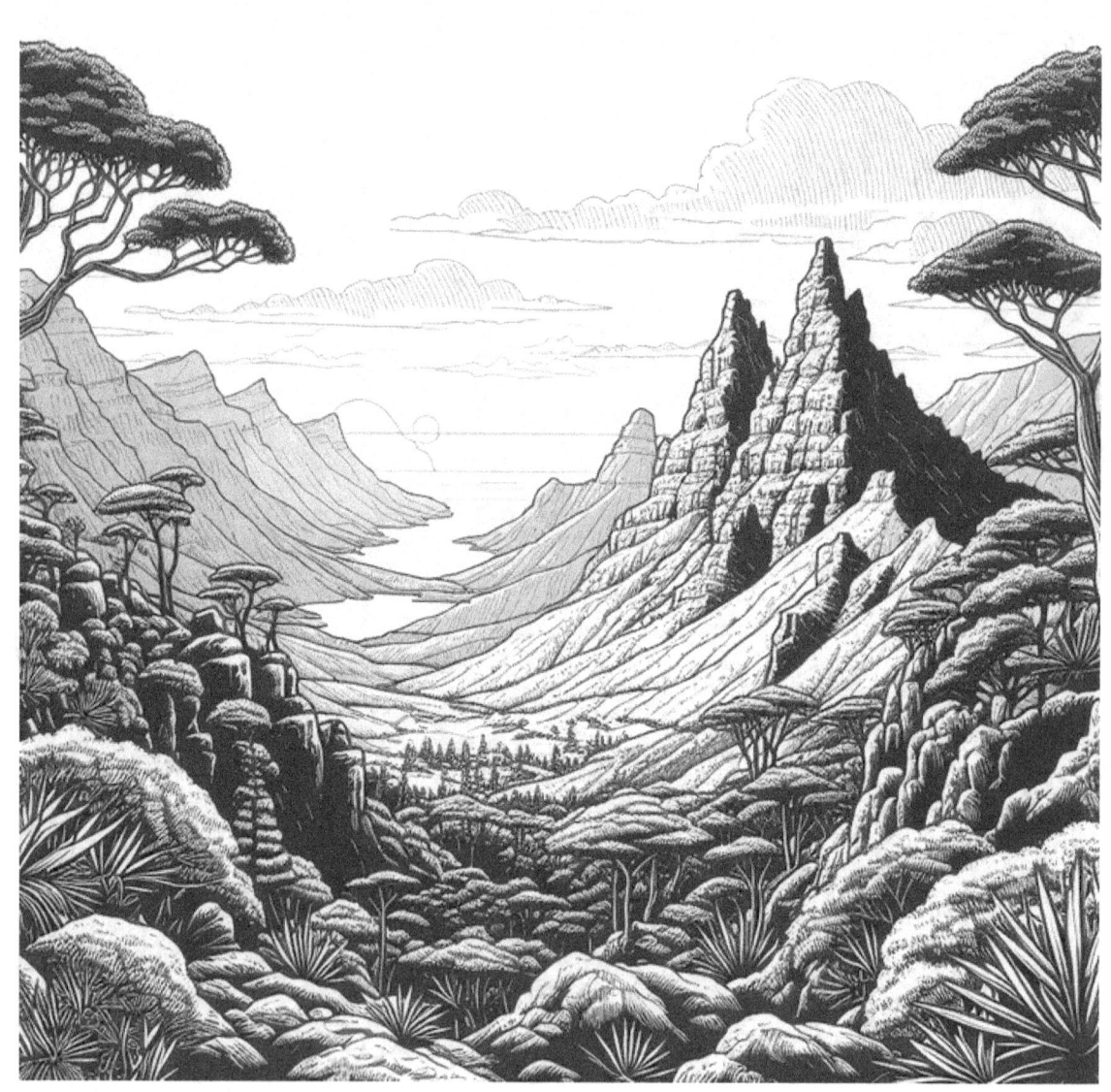

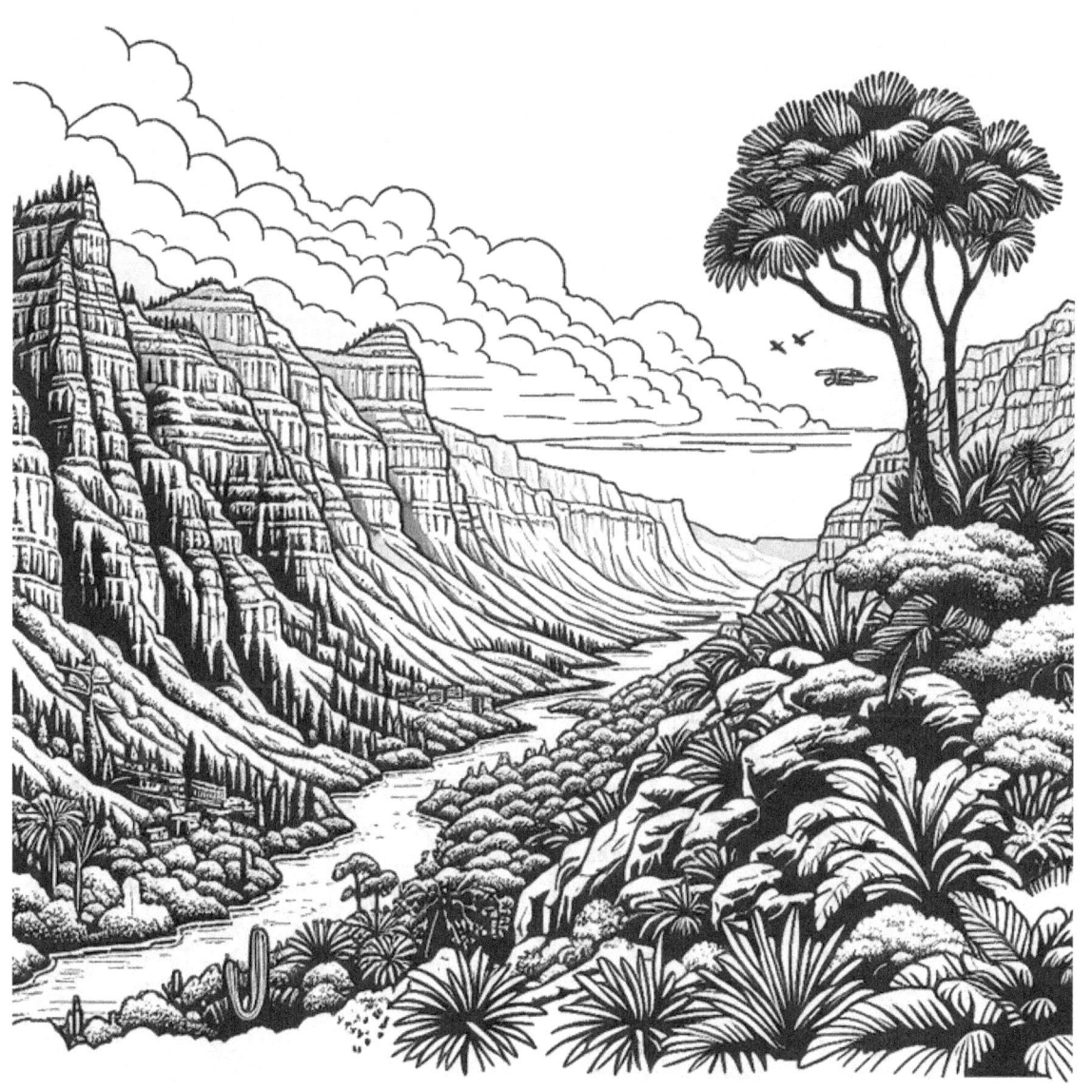

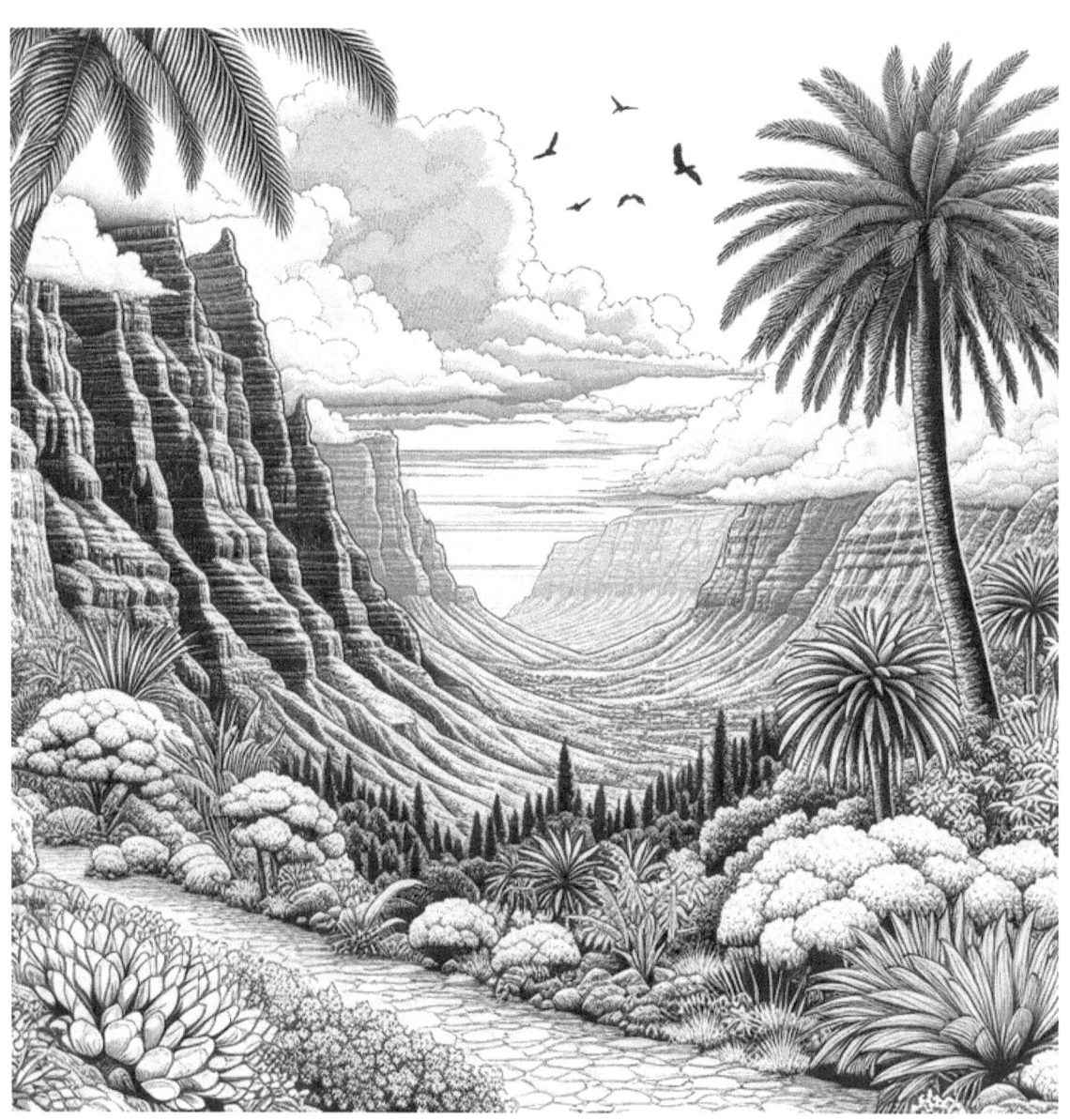

www.ingramcontent.com/pod-product-compliance
Lightning Source LLC
Chambersburg PA
CBHW062125220526
45471CB00010B/3882